On Lutes, Recorders
and Harpsichords

On Lutes, Recorders
and Harpsichords

Men and Music of the Baroque

Freda Pastor Berkowitz

DRAWINGS BY MALCOLM SPOONER

ATHENEUM *1967* *NEW YORK*

Copyright © 1967 by Freda Pastor Berkowitz
All rights reserved
Library of Congress catalog card number 67-18998
Published simultaneously in Canada by
McClelland & Stewart, Ltd.
Manufactured in the United States of America
Printed by The Murray Printing Company,
Forge Village, Massachusetts
Bound by H. Wolff, New York
First Edition

To my grandchildren

Table of Contents

On Lutes, Recorders
and Harpsichords

The Baroque Era

IT WAS THE END OF THE SIXTEENTH CENTURY. THE finely balanced, calm, classic art forms of the Renaissance were losing their hold over the minds of the creative artists of the day, especially those in Italy. A major change in attitude toward art and toward life itself was taking shape. In place of the evenly proportioned, carefully controlled art of the Renaissance, an art of restless opposition, of dramatic clashes, of strong passions, and of robust purposefulness was emerging.

The Baroque period had begun, and it would grow and flourish until the middle of the eighteenth century. It was to become a major period in the history of the arts. In the history of music it was an especially important period, for it was during this time that many of the musical forms we know today had their beginning.

The word "baroque" comes from the Portuguese word "barocco," meaning a large, irregularly shaped pearl. It was first applied to the architecture of the day, and it most probably was used to make fun of the new designs. Renaissance buildings had been built along simple, clean lines. Baroque buildings, on the other hand, were richly ornamented and dramatic. To persons unaccustomed to them, these early Baroque buildings seemed overdone and ostentatious—like the somewhat gaudy "barocco."

The freedom of design in Baroque architecture produced many magnificent buildings. Among the first and most famous Baroque buildings are Italian churches, such as the Church of the Gesu in Rome. A monument of great drama and power is the colonnades of St. Peter's Square in Rome, created by Giovanni Lorenzo Bernini, an architect and sculptor. From Italy Baroque ideas in architecture, and in the other arts, spread to France, Germany, and throughout Europe.

Painting and sculpture of the Baroque period also showed the dramatic, emphatic ideas of the times. No longer were paintings made up of equally balanced, separate elements. Now one strong element became the center of focus. Deep shadows, sharp diagonals, and rich, contrasting colors were used to give drama and singleness of purpose to the paintings of the day. A Flemish painter, Peter Paul Rubens, exemplifies the Baroque feelings about art in his works, which are rich in color and emotion. Rembrandt, too, seems Baroque in his deeply emotional paintings with their dramatic contrasts of dark and light. Bernini, in his passionate sculptures, also displays Baroque ideas.

The Baroque feeling in music can best be seen in the

colossal oratorios and other ensemble works of the period in which unequal masses of sound—solo and choral forces, vocal and instrumental colors—contend with one another. No longer were the evenly written, one-color compositions of the Renaissance popular. Instead, large and small volumes of contrasting sound were thrown back and forth. Drama and emotion replaced the calm, straightforwardness of Renaissance music. Simple music gave way to intricate and ornamental works. Baroque music was richly textured and dynamically expressive. It utilized dissonance and chromaticism as they had never been used before.

Of tremendous significance to music were the new forms, new styles, and highly developed instruments

SHAWM

that came into being during the Baroque period. Secular music for the first time since the fall of Rome became as important to serious musicians as religious music. Opera, with its emphasis on drama and emotion, grew out of the feelings of the period. By writing specific parts for specific instruments and by grouping certain types of instruments together, Baroque composers created the orchestra. New instruments were invented at this time and old ones perfected. New musical forms such as the sonata and concerto came into being in the Baroque period and have been used ever since.

In spite of the importance of the Baroque period in the development of music, many composers of the time and their works dropped into obscurity after the mid-eighteenth century. Only the two composers who climaxed the Baroque period—Johann Sebastian Bach and George Frederick Handel—were given much attention. However, in the past twenty-five years Baroque music and its beauty and importance have been once again recognized. This book contains descriptions of the lives and works of some of the most important Baroque composers who came before Bach and Handel.

Instruments of the Baroque

THE BAROQUE PREFERENCE FOR EXTREME CONTRASTS and strong emotion in music had a great influence on the musical instruments of the period. Musicians cried out for instruments that would express the gradations of tone color, the contrasts between light and dark, high and low, soft and loud, that they wanted to put into their music. Instrument makers, as a result, strove to provide deeper basses, more powerful and sensitive wind instruments, and instruments that would reproduce the tenderness, emotional expressiveness and range of the human voice.

New instruments have, of course, been developed since the Baroque period and many instruments used during that time have undergone a great deal of refinement over the years. But many are still used today in the same way they were in the Baroque period. Especially since the recent revival of interest in Baroque music have instruments of that period been in demand. What could be more sensible than to perform a Baroque composition on the instruments for which it was written?

The ancient RECORDER is one of the most popular instruments in the family of "whistle flutes." Its soft, thin sound can easily be compared to the voice of a bird. In fact, the word "recorder" comes from the old French verb which means "sing like a bird." In France the recorder is also called *flute à bec*, "flute with a beak," because its mouthpiece looks like the beak of a bird.

When the recorder player blows into his instrument, the air goes through a small channel in the beak-shaped mouthpiece to the edge of the sound hole and produces the sound. During the early part of the Baroque period there were several different sizes of recorders. Some were only a few inches long, while others were as long as four feet. The small recorders produced high sounds, the larger low sounds. Toward the end of the Baroque period when Johann Sebastian Bach wrote parts in his music for the recorder, he generally used one size. This recorder had a range of a little over two octaves, from the *F* above middle *C* to the *G* two octaves above. Bach referred to this instrument as the *flauto*.

After Bach's time the recorder was used very little. The people who arranged concerts discovered that it was more profitable to give concerts in larger rooms. So instruments with soft tones like the recorder had to be replaced with instruments that had stronger tones.

Not until the twentieth century was there a revival of interest in the recorder. The modern recorder is modeled after those used during the Baroque period, although it is often made of plastic today instead of wood or ivory. Modern recorders can generally be found in four sizes—soprano, alto, tenor, and bass.

Recently many young people and adults have become enthusiastic about learning to play the recorder. Perhaps this has come about because the instrument is inexpensive and not too difficult to learn. Much pleasure can be derived from playing the recorder as a solo instrument or with a group.

The BAROQUE FLUTE, or TRANSVERSE FLUTE, is made of wood and belongs to the same family as the recorder. It was given the name transverse flute to distinguish it from the recorder and because it is held in a horizontal position so that the player blows into a hole on the side of the instrument.

In 1677 Lully introduced the transverse flute into the orchestra. After that both recorders and transverse flutes were used in Baroque orchestras. Only the transverse flute is used in modern symphony orchestras. Today it is made of silver or metal instead of wood.

CORNETTS, or ZINKS as they were sometimes called, are not like our modern cornets. They are made of wood and resemble a trumpet. Their sound is as bright and clear as a human voice, and they were often used with voices in church choirs. Bach used cornetts to accompany a boys' choir in several of his cantatas. Today, in recordings of music by Monteverdi and Schütz, cornetts modeled after the Baroque instruments are used.

The trombone of the Baroque period is called the SACKBUT. It differs very little from the trombone used in modern symphony orchestras. It is a long, slender metal tube, bent several times in order to make it easy to hold. One of the parts of the tube is a slide. The sackbut player, like the trombonist of today, pushes the slide in and out to change the length of the tube. By doing this he is able to play all the notes in every scale—something that other brass instruments of the Baroque period can not do. The end of the sackbut, which is shaped like a bell, is smaller than the end of the modern trombone.

The sound of the sackbut is softer and less brassy than that of the modern trombone. Its soft sound made it an appropriate instrument for use in churches. It was a fine accompaniment for hymn tunes and chorales. Gabrieli, Schütz, Bach, and Handel all used the sackbut in their sacred music.

The first HORN to be used during the Baroque period was a kind of hunting horn—a pipe coiled in a circle large enough to carry over the shoulder. During the Baroque period it was used for the calls and fanfares of a royal hunt. One fanfare composed by Louis XV is still used for hunting parties today.

SHAWMS are antecedents of the oboes. During the Baroque period they were not constructed as carefully as later oboes and their tones are loud and raucous. Loudest of all instruments, except trumpets, they were used in military bands and in town bands for open air performances.

The OBOE followed the shawm in the middle of the seventeenth century. French craftsmen developed it into an instrument of delicate beauty, and it became an important instrument in the Baroque orchestra. Lully used the oboe in his operas, and Scarlatti, Vivaldi, Telemann, Bach, and Handel also used it in their works. Several of them wrote solo concertos for the oboe, which are still played today.

The KRUMMHORN is a wind instrument that looks like an oboe, except that it ends in a curve. Its name came from the German word "krumm," which means "curved." A pierced wind cap covers the reed of a krummhorn so a player cannot control the sound of his instrument by putting the reed directly into his mouth, as he can with an oboe. The soft and mournful sound made by the krummhorn was used little by musicians after 1617. In present day performances of early Baroque music, the krummhorn is sometimes used.

Often unwieldy in size, POMMERS are among the most impractical of the early instruments. They were made in various sizes, and one pommer—the great bass pommer—was a ten foot giant. It could not be played by one man; someone else had to be there to help him hold up his instrument. Pommers were sometimes called "bombards" because of the loud buzzing sound they made on the lower notes. For all this, pommers did serve a useful purpose. They are the ancestors of the more sonorous and practical bassoon.

The wind instrument with the lowest pitch is the BASSOON. It was developed during the Baroque period, in answer to the call for instruments which would provide strong contrasts in the form of deep, low notes. It can be traced back to the middle of the sixteenth century and was in general use by 1600. During the Baroque period it was employed most often to reinforce the bass stringed instruments of the orchestra. Handel was the first composer to use the bassoon as a solo instrument.

Because the tube of the Baroque bassoon is eight feet long, it is always bent in two. During the Baroque period the two loops of the tube were inserted in a small block of wood called the "butt," which was fitted with three keys. Today the bassoon has at least twenty-two keys. It is much easier to carry around because it now comes apart in five sections, or joints. The bassoon is often called the clown of the orchestra because of its loud, funny sound. But it can also play beautiful and serious music and is a valuable instrument in the modern symphony orchestra.

The RACKETT belongs to the bassoon family and is, indeed, a queer-looking instrument. It consists of a short, thick cylinder of solid wood pierced lengthwise by ten cylindrical channels which are connected to form a continuous tube. The sound of the rackett is quite the opposite of what one might expect. The rackett makes no racket at all, but instead makes a thin, reedy sound. In France this instrument was called the "sausage bassoon."

For centuries before the Baroque period the TRUMPET was used for military and ceremonial purposes. Only the court trumpeters were permitted to play the instrument. They announced the arrival of kings and summoned knights to battle. During the Baroque period, however, the trumpet became an important part of the orchestra. It was so important that guilds were formed that gave special privileges to the trumpet players. They received higher wages than any of the other musicians.

The Baroque trumpet is made of a long piece of metal tubing, which is bent into different shapes and sizes and spread at one end to form a bell. The other end of the instrument is fitted with a mouthpiece. There were two main types of trumpets: a small one called the "clarino," which plays high parts; and a larger one called the "principale," which plays lower parts. In some of Johann Sebastian Bach's works high and very difficult passages are written for the clarino. These passages cannot be played on the modern trumpet, so in performances today an instrument modeled after the clarino and called the "Bach trumpet" is used.

In accordance with the Baroque emphasis on the elaborate, many instruments of the time were heavily ornamented, and DRUMS were among the most elab-

DRUM

orate. Many were made of real silver. Some had hangings of costly embroidery. Often drummers in bands accompanied their performances with acrobatic exhibitions. However, drums were also used as serious instruments. Important parts for kettledrums appear in many scores of Bach and Handel.

Oldest of the stringed instruments is the LUTE. It is pear-shaped, has strings that are plucked by the fingers, and makes a gentle, restrained sound. By the Baroque period it had anywhere from twenty-six to thirty-three strings, the tuning and adjusting of which was a difficult and expensive job. An eighteenth century writer said, "I have been told that in Paris it costs as much to keep a lute as to keep a horse!"

A tenor lute, the theorbo, became popular during the Baroque period; Handel used it in many of his oratorios and operas.

The GUITAR came to Europe through the Moors in Spain. At first it had four double strings, but a fifth was later added. The pegs, which are used for tuning the instrument, were originally made of wood. In time the wooden pegs were replaced by metal screws. In the seventeenth century, when the guitar became a popular instrument, it was simplified; six single strings replaced the five double ones.

A Spanish guitarist of the Baroque period, Robert de Visée, became the guitarist at the court of Louis XIV. He started a rage for the guitar. Everyone from the ladies of the court to the stage comedians began strumming the guitar. Today the guitar has become a popular instrument once again.

An instrument so small that it could be tucked away in the flap pocket of a dancing master is the REBEC. It is a stringed instrument played with a bow like the violin and used mainly to indicate to dancing pupils the rhythm and melody of a piece of music.

During the early Baroque period the VIOL family was very popular. Its members—the treble viol, the tenor viol, and the bass viol, also known as the viola da gamba—are cousins of the violin. They have six thin strings and produce a subdued, rather nasal sound that was favored in the salons of nobility.

Many families, especially in England, owned a chest of viols. This was an actual chest in which a set, or consort, of the various sizes of viols was kept. Guests would often join in the playing of a consort of viols for an evening's entertainment.

When Baroque chamber music is performed today, viols like those of the Baroque period are often used so that the music will sound as it did at the time it was written. Originally viols were held downwards, resting on the knees. But today they are usually held the same way as a violin is held. The viola da gamba, however, is still held between the knees like a 'cello.

During the Baroque period great strides were made in the development of the VIOLIN. The most famous violin makers of the time lived in Cremona, Italy. Andrea Amati was the founder of the Cremona school of craftsmen. His grandson Niccolò Amati taught the art of violin making to Antonio Stradivari, who became one of the world's most famous violin makers. Stradivari's best pupil Joseph Guarneri del Gesù also produced fine instruments.

Even today violins made by Amati, Stradivari, and Guarneri are among the best in the world. Not long ago Isaac Stern, a great American violinist, was able to purchase a rare Guarneri violin. When he was asked how much he paid for his beautiful instrument, he jokingly said, "More than five dollars and less than $125,000." It was undoubtedly a costly purchase.

The viola and 'cello are also members of the violin family. The 'cello was a most useful instrument during the Baroque period. It was often used to provide the bass for the important *basso continuo.*

Members of the HARPSICHORD family were the important keyboard instruments of the Baroque period. They are the virginal, the spinet, and the harpsichord. All three worked in the same way. When the keys were pressed down, the strings inside the instruments were plucked by quills. This gave the instruments a thin, twangy sound.

The largest of the three instruments, the harpsichord, was also the most important. It was the major instrument for the execution of the *basso continuo* and was almost indispensable for the performance of orchestral music. Composers of the Baroque period usually conducted their works from the harpsichord.

In present times the harpsichord is once more coming into use. Much Baroque music is now performed on the harpsichord.

Some of the greatest music of the Baroque period was written for the ORGAN. Really two instruments in one, the organ is both a wind instrument and a keyboard instrument. Wind is needed to make the organ pipes sound. Tones are produced when wind is blown through the pipes. Each pipe sounds one note. There are often many sets of pipes, each set playing the notes of the scale in a different way: some mellow, some shrill, some very full, and even some like chimes. The organ has two separate keyboards to select the notes played: one operated by the hands, called the manual; the other operated by the feet, called the pedal keyboard. Buttons or levers called stops control which of the different sets of pipes are played.

Baroque organs are elaborate in construction. They have many sets of stops both for the manual and the pedal keyboards. Along with their complex construction, they are also most decorative. Some Baroque organs are the center of decoration for an entire church.

In addition to the large church organs, other smaller organs were used during the Baroque period. The positive organ, the tone of which is tender and gentle, was used in a chapel or music room. A portable instrument, the portative organ, was used for processions. The regal is still another type of organ. It was used primarily as an accompanying instrument. As early as 1619 Monteverdi used a regal in his opera *Orfeo*.

Giovanni Gabrieli

1557-1612

ST. MARK'S CATHEDRAL AND ITS SURROUNDING SQUARE, or piazza, was the center of public life in Venice in the sixteenth century. Work on the Cathedral, begun in the ninth and tenth centuries, had not really been completed until the 15th century. It had been a work of love, and the people were proud of what their ancestors had accomplished. The Cathedral, with its magnificent domes could be seen from long distances. The interior, filled with gold mosaics, paintings, and statues, inspired citizens and visitors alike with awe.

The Piazza of St. Mark's was the site of many state pageants and religious ceremonies. To these the people of Venice came in great numbers, delighting in the glory and greatness of the display.

It was into this city, and into a world where beauty and pageantry were so important, that Giovanni Gabrieli was born, perhaps in 1554, or more probably in 1557. No one knows for sure. It is known, however, that his family was an important one. His uncle, Andrea, was the leading composer, organist and teacher in Venice, and perhaps in all Italy. Musicians came from all over Europe to study with him.

When the young Gabrieli showed musical talent, he quickly became his uncle's pupil. He was taught singing, the fundamentals of composition, and how to play the organ. His uncle found him brilliant, so brilliant that by the time he was eighteen people were coming to Venice not only to study with Andrea Gabrieli, but also to hear Giovanni Gabrieli play.

The young Gabrieli's fame spread so rapidly that before he was nineteen he was offered a position as musical assistant to Orlando di Lasso at the court chapel in Munich. Di Lasso was considered to be the greatest Dutch musician of the sixteenth century, so the offer was not a small one. Gabrieli accepted and went to Munich. He stayed there for four years, acting as organist at the court chapel and composing madrigals and canzoni for local groups.

But Munich was not Venice, and the court chapel, though lovely, was not St. Mark's. Gabrieli longed for the familiar sights of Venice and the pageantry of his native city. So in 1579 he went home.

And it was truly to St. Mark's that he returned, for on January 1, 1580, he was appointed permanent second organist at the Cathedral. At the same time his uncle Andrea was made the first organist. Then when Andrea Gabrieli died in 1586, examinations were held to decide who should be his successor. Giovanni Gabrieli was of course one of the contestants. The examinations were hard, but he passed with little difficulty.

And so he became first organist at St. Mark's, a position he held until his death.

The composing that Gabrieli had been doing since his days in Munich was now all centered on making St. Mark's a place where the music equaled the beauty of the structure. This was both a challenge and an adventure for one as talented as Gabrieli, because St. Mark's offered him so many advantages for staging his music. For example, St. Mark's was built with two organ lofts, one on each side of the Cathedral. This made it possible to have two organs, two groups of singers, and two groups of instrumentalists. Because of this Gabrieli could achieve many grand effects, some of them possible in his time only in St. Mark's.

The Piazza of St. Mark's was also the site of musical performances. There was an altar in the Piazza where religious ceremonies could be held out of doors. The first of Gabrieli's group of "Sacred Symphonies" was composed for the coronation ceremonies for the wife of the Doge of Venice. This ceremony was held in the Piazza of St. Mark's.

Gabrieli composed continually. The "Sacred Symphonies," or *Sinfonia Sacrae,* when completed, consisted of sixty pieces for voices and instruments, set to various texts of the Church liturgy. The pieces were intended for use on special days of celebration in St. Mark's.

He also began writing motets. These are unaccompanied vocal compositions usually written for one chorus. But probably partly because Gabrieli could place groups in various places in St. Mark's, his were written for two, three, four or even five choruses. And these choruses, far from being unaccompanied, mingled with different instruments. Sometimes a solo voice created a special effect. Other times all the voices were joined together with the instruments for a big climax.

As he composed his motets, he was constantly looking for new devices that would make them even more interesting. In his motet *Timor and Tremor* ("Fear and Trembling") the words are set to music in such a way that it is possible to feel the "fear and trembling." To get this effect Gabrieli used dissonant chords, chords that make the listener tremble because the sound is not a pleasant one. And to make these dissonant chords even more impressive, he used them on the strong beats of the measure. In 4/4 time, for example, he used them on the first and third beats. To do this broke the rules of harmony in his day. But Gabrieli was not one to follow rules, when breaking them would achieve an effect he wanted.

Gradually, as Gabrieli experimented more and more with the motet, some of his works changed form so much that they could no longer be called motets. And when he began to use a small group of performers and then a larger one in the same composition to achieve contrast—something no one had thought of doing before—he had arrived at the beginning of an entirely new form. It later became very popular, and is known as the Concerto Grosso.

Gabrieli also laid the foundations of the modern orchestra. He was the first composer to group similar instruments together and to use certain instruments for special effects. For example, in his composition *Sonata Pian'e Forte,* the first part is written for a cornett and three trombones and the second for viol and three trombones. To achieve even more contrast and liveliness, Gabrieli used dynamic marks—*piano* meaning soft and *forte* meaning loud—on the written sheets of music. No one had ever done this before. It was such a new idea that Gabrieli called the piece *Sonata Pian'e Forte* because of the new markings.

In his compositions for instruments, Gabrieli was especially fond of brass. Perhaps this was because the brass instruments gave an impression of pomp and

HORN

splendor that matched the pomp and splendor he loved in Venice. When one listens to Gabrieli's *Music for Brass Choirs,* it is easy to imagine a procession of senators of the Republic of Venice dressed in long, elaborate, scarlet robes, walking from the Doge's Palace to the Cathedral.

Gabrieli's fame as an organist, composer and teacher spread to many countries. And people flocked from all over to St. Mark's. People had always come to Venice to hear music; it had been the musical center of Italy for a long time. But now many more came just to hear Gabrieli play and to hear his music performed in the Cathedral and in the Piazza. An English traveler visiting Venice wrote: "I heard the best music that ever I did in all my life that I would willingly goe a hundred miles a foote at any time to hear the like."

And of course, pupils came from all over Europe to study with the great master. He was a remarkable teacher. He was very strict and demanded a great deal from his pupils, but they, because they learned so much from him, loved him and willingly did all he asked.

Gabrieli's most accomplished student was Heinrich Schütz. He came from Germany to study with Gabrieli for two years but was so impressed with Gabrieli's teaching that he remained in Venice for three. Schütz later became an outstanding German composer. In his later life Schütz always remembered his teacher. At one time he said, "I went to spend the first years of my apprenticeship with the great Gabrieli! Immortal Gods! What a man this Gabrieli! If a Goddess were looking for a husband, she would want no other husband than he. So great is he in the art of music."

Gabrieli also loved Schütz and foresaw a great future for his pupil. At one time Gabrieli gave his most precious ring to Schütz, and Schütz never parted with it.

Although Gabrieli had tempting offers from royalty in Germany to visit and work in that country again, he was never able to bring himself to leave his pupils and his beloved city of Venice. During the last ten years of his life, he was not well. Many times his pupils, and especially Schütz, had to substitute for him in St. Marks. He died in August, 1612, and was buried in Venice, in the church of Saint Etienne. He was mourned by pupils and friends all over Europe.

At the time of his death he was, and still is, considered to be one of the greatest masters of church music that has ever lived. His choral works have never been surpassed. Truly he did bring to the music of St. Mark's the same glory that its architects and fine artists had brought to its appearance.

Today Gabrieli's works are performed all over the world, though it was only in 1965 that a complete edition of his works was assembled. Among them were madrigals, canzoni, motets, masses, works for brass choirs, organ works, the *Sinfonia Sacra* and the *Sonata Pian'e Forte*.

In some places where these works are being performed today, attempts are being made to duplicate the conditions Gabrieli must have envisioned for them in St. Mark's. At a recent performance of his choral work *Benedictus*, which is written for three choruses and brasses, the choruses and instruments were placed in three different parts of the stage. The sound was like magic! And this may well be just the way the music sounded in Gabrieli's time when the performers were arranged in the different organ lofts of St. Mark's.

Similarly, in a recent recording of a composition for brass instruments called the *Seven Canzoni* the instruments were placed at opposite ends of the recording studio. The conductor was placed midway between them. Again the sound was like magic!

In Gabrieli's day, a traveler went to St. Mark's to hear the music of the master performed as it should be performed; but today, perhaps we are able to hear the works as he planned them to be and in the true spirit of the early Baroque, wherever we may be.

Don Carlo Gesualdo,

Prince of Venosa

1560-1613

Gesualdo, the Prince of Venosa
Was a truly astounding composer
Though much of his history
Is shrouded in mystery
We have here all the facts we do know Sir.

IN THE SIXTEENTH CENTURY, AS IN THE CENTURIES
before it, what most men became in life was determined
by their birth. That is, the son of a farmer became a
farmer, the son of a shoemaker became a shoemaker,
and the son of a prince became a prince. This was
especially true for the oldest son in the family. But for
almost all children, education and opportunities for
achievement were almost entirely determined by the
family they belonged to.

To most people it must have seemed that the best kind of family to be born into was a noble family, for here one was more likely to have a chance to do what one wanted to do. The duties and responsibilities of the nobles were not too heavy. They had plenty of money, generally, to maintain themselves, and many opportunities for education and adventure were open to them that were not open to other people. But although all of these things were true, then as now, money and birth did not always mean a happy life. Don Carlo Gesualdo was an example of a case where it did not.

He was born in 1560, the second son of one of the oldest and noblest families in all Italy. His father was a prince, his ancestors had been princes, lords, counts, warriors and statesmen. One of his uncles, Alfonso, was Cardinal Archbishop of Naples.

With such a background it seemed likely that his life would be full of peace and pleasantness. But such was not the case, although in the beginning his life was happy. This was especially so because he loved music. All the Gesualdos were fond of music. And because they were a noble family, they had the time and money to have as much of it as they liked. Fabrizio, Don Carlo's father was an amateur composer. He was anxious that his child know as much about music as possible and was overjoyed when he realized that Don Carlo showed musical talent.

In order that Don Carlo might hear a great deal of music, the prince established a musical academy right in his own home. This was known as a "camerata." The best musicians in Venosa came to live with the Gesualdo family and were always available to play for the family or to teach.

Among these musicians was Pomponio Nenna. He was a well-known composer of madrigals and a fine teacher. He taught Don Carlo how to play several instruments including the guitar and the lute.

More important, Nenna taught Don Carlo how to compose madrigals. This was an important kind of song in that day. Madrigals had originally been a specific kind of poem, containing a set number of lines, each of a specific length. Some of these poems were eventually set to music, and the songs that resulted became known as madrigals. Over the years the form of the poem and the music to which it was set changed, but the name madrigal remained.

The music for a madrigal was elaborate, with several voices or parts, each sung by at least two or three people. The harmonies between the voices and the development of the melodies sung by the different voices were often very complex.

Gesualdo seems to have enjoyed working on madrigals, for he learned well the basic skills he needed to compose them. But this was not all he was interested in. He played several instruments, and as he grew older, he surrounded himself with musicians and poets. The poets supplied the words for the madrigals he wrote.

Don Carlo's favorite poet was Tarquato Tasso. Often Gesualdo went to his castle, St. Antonio in Mergellina, just outside of Naples, taking Tasso with him. There the two would spend whole nights out in the Bay of Naples singing madrigals and villotas. The villota was a folk song with a dancelike rhythm.

In this happy manner the first twenty-five years of his life passed. Then Gesualdo's older brother Luigi died, and Gesualdo became heir to the many titles and to the vast estates of the Gesualdo family. Since he and his brother had been the only sons in the family, Gesualdo was now the only heir. There was no one to take his place if he should die. It was important for a noble family to have an heir, so Don Carlo's duty was clearly to marry and have a son.

In 1586, when Gesualdo was twenty-six, a marriage was arranged for him with his first cousin, Donna Maria d'Avalos. Donna Maria was a beautiful woman, but she was frivolous. The family felt, however, that once she was married to Don Carlo, she would take life more seriously. The marriage was a happy one for a few years. A son, Emanuele, was born and the need for an heir was fulfilled. So for Don Carlo life was full of good things, just as he might have expected.

But then early in 1590, Donna Maria gave in to her frivolous nature and fell in love with a handsome duke. At first Don Carlo was not aware of this. Then one day he returned home unexpectedly from a hunting expedition to find Donna Maria with her lover. Don Carlo was overcome with jealousy and in a mad frenzy killed them both.

Although the son of a noble family (and the heir to great titles could do many things that others could not) Don Carlo had gone too far. Punishment for such a crime, in that day and under those circumstances, was not likely as far as the government was concerned. But the relatives of the dead wife and her lover were almost sure to seek revenge. Gesualdo's first thought was to run away, and the viceroy of the town, Don Giovanni Zuniga, agreed that this was wise.

Gesualdo wasted no time. The refuge he chose was his country castle, Gesualdo. It was situated about 180 miles east of Naples. But even at that distance he was afraid. He had the castle heavily fortified, and he cut down the forest and thickets around the castle, so nothing would obstruct his view in case his enemies were suddenly to appear.

Gesualdo kept himself locked up for about two years. And the only way he was able to forget his fear was to practice the lute and to compose madrigals. It was an unhappy time for him, and for his family.

LUTE

During the time that Don Carlo kept himself a prisoner in his castle, he received word that his father had died. Don Carlo, himself, was now "Prince of Venosa." He began to wonder how long he could keep himself locked up and became very restless. He wanted to return to Venosa and be accepted once more by society. So through his uncle, the Archbishop, he began to negotiate with the families of Donna Maria and her lover, and eventually he was forgiven and permitted to return to Venosa.

Gesualdo's uncle even arranged another marriage for him. This time with Eleanora d'Este, the daughter of the Duke of Ferrera. Gesualdo was glad and wasted no time in Venosa. He immediately began to make preparations for the trip to Ferrera.

Because the trip was to be a long one Don Carlo took a complete caravan with him. There were many musicians, courtiers, and servants in his party, as well as twenty-four baggage mules carrying over three hundred boxes of supplies. The party probably left Venosa about Christmas of 1593. Ferrera was about three hundred miles north of Venosa, and the trip undoubtedly took several weeks. One of the musicians of the group kept a diary of the journey:

> Gesualdo rises late. He is unpunctual. We do not know whether it is because he works at night at his composing or does not sleep well. He is melancholy. He likes to hunt. He is ceremonious in manner and fastidious in dress. And like most musicians likes to discourse at great length on the subject of his art.
>
> He can never have enough music. He had with him a great many books in five parts. All his own. He had only four people who could sing. He sang the fifth part. If he didn't sing, he accompanied on the guitar. He also played the lute. In his new music Gesualdo is writing in a different style.

When Don Carlo and his caravan arrived in Ferrera, sometime early in 1594, the whole city was jubilant about the wedding. The castle of Ferrera was alive with excitement. The wedding itself and the festivities lasted for a whole week.

Eleanora proved to be a fine woman and a devoted wife. Soon the Gesualdos had a son and Don Carlo was once again settled and happy. He and his wife did not return to Venosa but remained in Ferrera. It was an ideal city for Gesualdo to live in because it was full of musical activity. Once more, he was enjoying the full life his birth gave him a right to expect.

There were as many as three or four concerts a day in the palace of the Grand Duke of Ferrera. Sometimes as many as fifty-seven singers took part in one concert. And not only did trained musicians take part in these concerts, but the noblemen themselves participated.

Music was such an important part of the life of the palace that eminent professors were engaged to teach the noblemen, their children, and even the pages and the gentlemen-in-waiting. The music library in the palace is said to have been the most extensive one in existence at that time. Instruments were made right there, and special musicians were hired to keep them in tune.

But it was not in the palace alone that music held such an important place. The nunneries in Ferrera were also important musical centers. The nuns had musical duties as well as religious ones. Musical evenings were often held at the nunneries, and the whole court was invited. Some of the nuns sang, others played the viols and the organs, and still others composed music.

In such an atmosphere Gesualdo seemed to find

great inspiration. There were many important composers at the court, and he was not by any means the least among them. In fact, he was considered the greatest composer of madrigals of his time. And it was in the years following his marriage to Eleanora that he did his best work.

Don Carlo's first and second books of madrigals were published in 1594, his third in 1595, his fourth in 1596, and his fifth and sixth in 1611. Altogether he composed one hundred and forty-seven madrigals.

In his madrigals he used new and what were considered daring harmonies. He was the first composer to use chromaticism in his harmonies. Chromaticism occurs when a composer uses notes in a work that are not the ones in the regular major and minor scale of the key in which the piece is written. For example, in the key of C major there are no sharps or flats. But Don Carlo might use chords with F# or D# or any note he wanted to in a madrigal written in C major, even though these notes did not belong to the key.

In many of his madrigals he did what he called "word painting." This was also new. If the words were "an angel ascended to heaven," the music ascended higher and higher with the words.

When Gesualdo published his madrigals, he put all the parts for all the different voices together in one volume. Before this, each part of the madrigal had been published in a different volume. There would be one volume for sopranos, one for altos, and so on. This made it difficult for the singers to know what others were doing. Don Carlo's idea was such a good one, it has been used ever since. Most musical scores today have all the parts, whether for singers or instruments, in one volume.

The happy days of musical activity in Ferrera came to an end when Eleanora's father died in 1597. The city then came under the rule of the Pope, and music was restricted to the Church. After a year or two of this, Gesualdo and his family went to Naples. But Don Carlo's days of happiness were over. The years in Naples were not good ones. The Gesualdos' only son suddenly became very ill and died. The son by his first marriage had also died. And Don Carlo, himself, was not well. At times he felt as if he were going mad. He imagined that demons were after him to punish him for the crimes that he had committed. He even engaged ten or twelve men "to beat the demons out of him."

The only time Gesualdo knew peace was when he was composing. But now his madrigals were full of sadness. These are the words to one of his best known madrigals "Moro Lasso" or "Weary unto Death," written in 1611:

> *I die Alas! for my pain,*
> *And who can give me life*
> *Alas, kills me and will not*
> *Give me life . . .*

But even in his time of grief he was able to invent new and striking harmonies. In the opera *Die Walküre* written by the German composer, Richard Wagner, in 1857, almost 250 years later, there are a few measures of chromatic chords exactly like the beginning of Gesualdo's "Morro Lasso."

Finally after much suffering Don Carlo, Prince of Venosa, died in 1613. He was hailed in death, as in life, as the "Prince of Composers." This was not only because of his title, but also because of his great contributions to music.

In our day Gesualdo's madrigals are performed all over the world. His daring harmonies and the beauty of his music do not sound revolutionary to us, but they do not sound old-fashioned either.

Igor Stravinsky, one of the great composers of our time, arranged several of Gesualdo's madrigals as music for a ballet. This was called "Momentum pro Gesualdo," and it was first performed in New York City in 1960 by the New York Ballet Company.

Claudio Monteverdi

1567-1643

THE TIME WAS BETWEEN 1585 AND 1600. THE PLACE was Florence, Italy. And the participants were a group of musicians, poets, and scholars called the "Camerata." They met in the palace of the poet Giovanni Bardi to discuss how they could change the musical style of the day. Tired of madrigals, they wanted to experiment with something different, a new kind of music for the human voice.

At first the group discussed reviving the ancient Greek solo song. But this did not seem to be different enough. The Camerata met again and again. Idea after idea was put forth and cast aside.

One member of the group, Vincenzo Galilei, father of Galileo Galilei, finally suggested that it might be more effective to have a single voice declare the singer's love or bewail his fate, rather than to have a group do it together, as was done in madrigals.

Seizing on this idea, Jacopo Peri, another member of the group and a musician, suggested that perhaps there might be a style of singing that imitated speaking to help tell a story. Still other members of the group thought it would be a good idea to have a small orchestra accompany singers. And to make musical performances even more interesting, it was decided that the singers might wear costumes and sing before a painted background that would suggest appropriate scenery.

A new form of musical display had been born. In 1597 Jacopo Peri took all of these new ideas and composed music for the first opera. The singer sang his feelings in an aria. The singer told his story in a recitative. In between the story was taken up by groups of singers that became a chorus.

The first opera that Peri wrote was called *Daphne*. It was a great success and gradually the reputation of the Camerata and of Peri spread all over Europe. The idea of opera became so popular that in 1600 King Henry IV of France commissioned Peri to compose a special opera to celebrate his coming marriage to Marie de Medici. Peri composed one called *Euridici* for the occasion, and it was very well received. But the form was still in the experimental stage. No one had yet written a really great opera. That waited for the genius of one man, Claudio Monteverdi.

Monteverdi was born and grew up long before the Camerata began meeting in Florence. But he was not a part of the group, for he lived in Cremona, Italy, in Milan, and in Mantua.

He was born in Cremona on May 15, 1567. Like many Italian cities of the time, Cremona was a musical place. It was a center for the making of fine musical instruments, and in the seventeenth and eighteenth centuries, it became especially famous for the marvelous Amati, Guarneri and Stradivari violins made there.

Monteverdi's father was a well-known doctor and a highly cultured man. Music was one of his great interests. He and his wife encouraged all of their children to study music and were delighted when Claudio and his younger brother, Giulo Cesare, showed talent.

Thus Claudio's musical education began early. He was a student in the choir school of the cathedral by the time he was ten or twelve. His first teacher was Antonio Ingegneri, who not only taught him to sing but also to play the organ and the viola and to compose music.

At the same time, Claudio attended the university, which stood in the heart of the city. He studied history, mathematics and literature and is said to have excelled in the classics and been able to recite many of Plato's works by heart.

Claudio's dual interest in literature and in music may have led him into an interest in madrigals, although they were such an important kind of music at the time that most young musicians tried writing them. At any rate, by the time he was eighteen, his first book of madrigals had already been published. His next composition, "Canzonetta in Three Voices," published when he was nineteen, still exists and shows remarkable talent. And the following year his book of madrigals for five voices indicated his true genius.

With these accomplishments already behind him, at the age of twenty Monteverdi decided to go to Milan. Because it was a larger city than Cremona, he hoped it would offer more opportunities. And indeed it did, for he had been in the city only a short time when the Duke of Mantua heard of him and invited him to come to Mantua as a violist, singer, and composer.

Monteverdi left for Mantua at once. His job there consisted of playing the viola in the court orchestra, composing madrigals and taking part in the singing of them.

It was while a group was rehearsing one of his madrigals that he met a young singer, Claudia Cattaneo. Her father was violist in the court orchestra, just as Monteverdi was. The two, Monteverdi and Claudia, were soon in love, and at the end of 1594 they were married.

Only a few months later the Duke summoned Monteverdi to accompany him and his army to Hungary. They were going there to fight against the Turks. Claudio was not expected to fight, but was put at the head of a group of musicians who were to entertain the Duke in the evenings when the day's fighting was over.

The campaign against the Turks was unsuccessful and everyone was glad when it was over. Monteverdi could not get home soon enough to suit him. There he had some of the madrigals that he had composed in Hungary published. These madrigals were full of new ideas. The harmonies and the chords were strange and new to those who heard them. Some critics of the time objected to them. One of the worst critics was the monk Giovanni Artusi who said that Monteverdi's madrigals were written with "dissonances that offended the ear." He also said that the madrigals were "careless and radical" and that "good musicians should have nothing to do with them."

At first Monteverdi was disturbed by this criticism.

But he had great confidence in his ideas, and he felt that he had really contributed something to the development of music. Fortunately most other musicians agreed with him. And the Duke of Mantua, too, thought Monteverdi's madrigals were wonderful. He gave Monteverdi the title "Master of Musicians."

Early in 1600 Claudia gave birth to the Monteverdi's first child, Francesco. When his son was born, Monteverdi felt that he needed a better position and more money. He had heard that the head of music at the court was about to retire, so he wrote a formal letter to the Duke applying for the position. The Duke was busy with affairs of state, and it took about a year before Monteverdi's request was granted. But finally Monteverdi was made the new head of music at the court of Mantua.

In his new position, Monteverdi was in charge of all of the singers and players at the court. Since the Duke required many performances for himself and his friends, Monteverdi had to compose new madrigals at an incredible rate. Beside all this, he also had to teach music to the children of the court as well as the singers.

Even though so much was expected of Monteverdi, he never received his salary on time. The jewelers and the tailors and everyone else who worked at the court were paid before the musicians. Monteverdi was constantly worried about how he would pay his bills.

The Duke, however had plenty of money for other things. He traveled and spent lavishly wherever he went. In 1603 he invited Monteverdi to join him on a vacation to Spa in Flanders. Spa was a fashionable resort where the Duke was to take mineral baths for his health and have a pleasant time with the other nobles who were there.

Unlike the trip to Hungary, this was a journey Monteverdi relished. Music was one of the favorite amusements in Spa. Traveling musicians flooded the place in order to entertain the visitors. The musicians sang songs in different languages and accompanied themselves on guitars and lutes. It was an opportunity to meet musicians and hear new works from many different lands. It was probably in Spa, then, that Monteverdi first heard the light, gay music of the French court. He was charmed and began at once to compose in a lighter style. His first such compositions were called "Scherzi Musicali." A scherzo is a lively, humorous piece.

It was probably in Spa, too, that Monteverdi first became really familiar with opera. For by 1603 this new form was spreading rapidly and operas were undoubtedly performed in Spa that year. Monteverdi may have heard of them before, but he probably had had no first hand contact with musicians who had played and sung in them, much less composed them.

Eventually the Duke of Mantua heard of these developments, too. No doubt envious of others who had such music at their command, he soon ordered Monteverdi to write an opera for him. And Monteverdi was ready and eager to do so.

All of Monteverdi's early training now came to bear on his new musical adventure. His early love of literature provided him with stories and an ear for poetry. And his long work with madrigals had taught him vocal harmonies and the work to which a human voice could be put. He set to work at once on his first opera *Orfeo*. In it he introduced many new ideas. Besides arias, duets, and choruses, Monteverdi used an orchestra of forty players. Up until this time only a few lutes, a harpsichord and a viola da gamba had been used as an instrumental accompaniment. Monteverdi used flutes, cornetts, trumpets, trombones and stringed instruments.

CELLO

Not only did Monteverdi use many different instruments, but he used them in a completely new way. He let certain instruments help to express certain moods. The recorders were good for pastoral scenes. The trombones and cornetts produced an eerie effect that suited the scenes of the mythological underworld. Trumpets and drums were good for battle scenes. Flutes and oboes sounded best for quiet moods. The viols, tender and sweet, were excellent for passages about love. And the harps and lutes made one think of heaven.

When the first performance of *Orfeo* was held on February 22, 1607, in the court of the Duke of Mantua, it was a tremendous success. The first operatic masterpiece had been written.

The great success of *Orfeo* pleased Monteverdi, but it did not allay a great unhappiness. Claudia had not been well since she had given birth to their second son, Massimiliano, in December of 1604. Because she had been growing steadily worse, she decided to take her two boys to Cremona to see if Monteverdi's father could help her. Unfortunately nothing could be done for her, and she died on September 10, 1607. Monteverdi was beside himself with grief. But he had little time to dwell on his sorrow. Because *Orfeo* had been such a success, the Duke demanded another opera immediately. Monteverdi set to work on one called *Arianna*. When it was finished, it was beautiful, but sad. No doubt Monteverdi was thinking of his own tragedy while he was composing it.

Arianna was first performed in May of 1608 to celebrate the wedding of the son of the Duke of Mantua. An immense theater was especially built for the performance and six thousand people attended. Accounts written at the time say that when the heroine, Arianna, sang her aria "Let Me Die," the whole audience was in tears. "Let Me Die," or "Arianna's Lament" as it is sometimes called, was the first great operatic aria.

After the first performance of *Arianna*, Monteverdi was completely exhausted. Not only was he in ill health, but he was worried about money. The Duke was behind in the payment of his salary as usual.

This time Monteverdi decided to leave Mantua. He took his two sons and went to visit his father in Cremona. Monteverdi's father was upset about his son's situations. He immediately wrote a touching letter to the Duchess of Mantua explaining the unfortunate condition of his gifted son, Claudio. The Duchess must have been moved by this letter, for she insisted that her husband do something to help Monteverdi. The Duke promised to give Monteverdi a regular amount of money each month if he would return to Mantua. So at the end of September, 1609, Monteverdi and his sons went back.

It took Monteverdi some time to get settled, and it was not until 1610 that he began to compose again. Most of his new works were religious. After a time he assembled all of these in one beautiful volume, which he dedicated to Pope Paul V. He took the works to Rome himself, hoping that the Pope would help him get his volume published. But unfortunately the Pope could not do this, and Monteverdi returned to Mantua disappointed.

No sooner had Monteverdi returned to Mantua than he had an even greater disappointment. Both the Duke and the Duchess of Mantua died suddenly. Their eldest son, Prince Francesco, ascended the throne and the first thing he did was to dismiss Monteverdi. This was most unjust, and no one knew the reason for it.

Monteverdi was completely discouraged. The only thing he could do was take his sons and once more return to his father's house in Cremona. After twenty-one years of service in Mantua, all he had was twenty-one scudi jingling in his pockets.

For about a year after that, Monteverdi was unable to find any position at all. It was fortunate for him that his father was able to support him. Then in 1613 the head of music of St. Mark's Cathedral in Venice died, and Monteverdi was chosen to be his successor.

On October 12, 1613, Monteverdi, his two sons and a few companions set out for Venice. But still misfortune seemed to accompany him. This is part of a letter he wrote to his friend Striggio:

> I beg to inform your Honour that while I was in the company of the Mantua Courier on my way to Venice we were set upon unawares by three ruffians and robbed in San Guanato or rather not in the place itself but a good two miles away. It happened on this wise: From a a field by the side of the road, one of the rascals, dark hued with sparse beard and of medium height, carrying a long musket with the trigger cocked, suddenly emerged, and another came forward and threatened me with his musket, while the third grasped the bridle of my horse, which continued on its way quite unconcerned and without showing resistance— and led it into the field. I was quickly dismounted and made to go down on my knees, while one of the two armed men demanded my purse. They then seized everything they could, crammed it into a huge bundle, hoisted it on their backs and made off with it . . . I had a half year's pay coming to me and if you would be so good as to put in a favorable word for me I should be most deeply grateful, for I stand in sore need . . .

Once in Venice, however, Monteverdi's luck seemed to change. He loved Venice. The people there seemed happier than those in Mantua. When Monteverdi walked along the narrow streets and heard the gay laughter coming from the people on the canal, he, too, was happy.

There was much work to be done at St. Mark's. There had been a lapse in time since there had been a director of music and the singers and the musicians were completely disorganized. In a short time he had restored discipline and order. He engaged good singers, and he saw to it that they learned many pieces of church music, both old and new. His accomplishments were so much appreciated that his salary was increased. For once in his life he did not have to worry about money.

Now, to his joy, Monteverdi was able to provide a good education for his sons. He planned that Francesco should become a lawyer and Massmiliano a doctor. Massmiliano eventually went to Bologna to study medicine. And in time he became one of the best doctors in Mantua. But although Francesco started out with the idea of becoming a lawyer, he changed his mind and became a Carmelite friar. Since he had a fine voice, he became one of the leading tenors of St. Mark's. Though Monteverdi had hoped for a lawyer, he was glad to have his son near him.

Besides composing works for St. Mark's, Monteverdi was also asked to compose an opera for the court in Parma, and a new book of madrigals for the court in Mantua. Then in 1624 he was commissioned to compose music for a scene from the poet Tasso's *Jerusalem*. The scene chosen was called *Il Combattimento di Tancredi e Clorinda* ("The Battle Between Tancredi and Clorinda"). It celebrated a battle fought in Jerusalem during the Crusades. The warrior, Tancredi, was a crusader and his opponent Clorinda, a pagan. They fought an exciting duel on horseback. And it was only after Tancredi had killed Clorinda and lifted the helmet of his opponent that he realized that Clorinda had been a beautiful woman and not at all the fierce warrior he had thought he was fighting.

Monteverdi's music was as exciting as the story. For the first time he used what is called a "tremolo." This is done by drawing the bow of a stringed instrument rapidly to and fro across a string on one note. The tremolo is still used by composers today to make music sound exciting. This was a part of Monteverdi's new style that was to bring something new not only to opera but to all music. Called *stillo concitato,* his new approach to sound emphasized excitement and other effects that made his music seem alive.

Monteverdi also used the pizzicato for the first time. This is done by plucking the strings of the instruments instead of drawing the bow across them. Monteverdi used this effect to imitate the clashing sounds of the swords. He used repetition of chords to imitate the galloping of horses.

Unfortunately in the midst of this happy and productive time, terrible things began to happen in Venice. First, the city was plundered by the Germans and valuable things were destroyed. Among these were many of Monteverdi's manuscripts. Then the great plague hit the city in July of 1630. The disease raged on for sixteen months, and forty thousand people perished. When finally on November 28, 1631, the plague was officially declared to be over, a solemn mass composed by Monteverdi was performed in St. Mark's Cathedral.

Monteverdi was so grateful that he and his sons had

been spared that he decided to become a priest. In 1632 he received his orders of priesthood. However, he kept right on with his teaching and composing. He finished his eighth book of madrigals and started to write a book on the theory of music. When he reached his seventieth birthday in May of 1637, he was working harder than ever. And in fact, he was tremendously excited about a new development in Venice that might let him return to his greatest love, opera.

It was in 1637 that the first public opera house, the Teatro di Cassiano, was built in Venice. Before this time opera was performed only for invited audiences in the palaces of kings, dukes and princes. But anyone who bought a ticket was admitted to a performance in the Teatro di Cassiano.

The operas were performed in a most elaborate way. Architects were hired to make gigantic scenery. Costumes were made of luxurious velvets, satins, and rich brocades. And the musicians and singers were brought from every corner of Italy. But the only light in the Teatro di Cassiano came from the elaborate candelabras on the stage. And these were more for decoration than light. So in order to make it possible for people to find their seats, small candles, or "cerinos", were sold at the door.

Old though he was, Monteverdi composed five new operas for the Teatro di Cassiano. Unfortunately only two of these have remained. *The Return of Ulysses to His Fatherland,* and *The Coronation of Poppea.* The latter was Monteverdi's last and greatest opera. It was given its first performance at the Teatro di Cassiano in 1642.

The Coronation of Poppea was the first historical opera. Up until that time, operas had been based on subjects in Greek mythology. But *The Coronation of Poppea* was about the Emperor Nero and Imperial Rome. The people of Venice loved splendor and intrigue. So they were thrilled as they watched and listened to the opera. The music was full of excitement and the spirit of youth. It was hard to believe that it had been written by a man of seventy-four.

After the great success of his opera, Monteverdi felt weary for the first time. His one desire was to visit the places which he had known as a boy. So he spent six months away from Venice, visiting Cremona and Mantua.

When he returned to Venice in the autumn of 1643, he became ill. And after twenty days of fever, he died on November 29, 1643. Monteverdi had worked hard and he had accomplished a great deal. He had done more new things than any other composer of his time. The body of work he left behind was enormous. Only in the beginning of the twentieth century was it all finally put together. The Italian composer, Malipiero, collected and made a complete edition of all the works of Monteverdi still in existence. Among these are the beautiful "Arianna's Lament," sections of his first opera *Orfeo,* and all of *The Return of Ulysses to His Fatherland,* and *The Coronation of Poppea* and many madrigals and canzonettas. These works are still performed all over the world.

Girolamo Frescobaldi

1583-1643

THE BAROQUE PERIOD WAS A TIME OF IMPATIENCE. The old was passing and something new and exciting was beginning. Everywhere people were experimenting with new ideas, and musicians were no exception. Never content with what had been done before, they were constantly looking for new harmonies, new forms of music, and new instruments.

One of the oldest instruments, and yet one of the newest in the Baroque Period was the organ. There had been organs of one sort or another since the third century B.C. But not until the thirteenth century did the organ have a real keyboard, and not until the fifteenth and sixteenth centuries, the Baroque Period, did it have all of the many effects we know in the organ today.

In those times people interested in music had to

work hard just to keep up with all that was being done and all that was being invented. And they had to begin their musical training early in order to have background enough to keep up with the things that were happening.

It helped a potential musician to have his ability recognized early and to begin his training soon. Fortunately this was the case for Girolamo Frescobaldi. He was born in Ferrara, Italy, an Italian city that was bursting with music. Even as a very small boy, he was intensely aware of music; he was always singing himself and eager to know all that people would tell him about music.

Because the city was musical, Frescobaldi's parents had many people around them they could turn to for advice on the training of their son, once they had discovered how talented he was. Ferrera was ruled by the D'Este family, whose love of music was so great that there were sometimes as many as three or four concerts a day in the palace of the Grand Duke of D'Este. It was to some of these musicians that Frescobaldi's parents went for advice, and consequently the young Frescobaldi received the best possible musical training.

His first teacher was Luzzaschi Luzzasco, considered to be one of the finest musicians of the time. In addition to teaching and composing, he was the organist and Grand Director of Music for the D'Este Ducal Chapel and was also organist of the cathedral in Ferrara.

Luzzasco was delighted with his pupil. He taught the boy to play the organ, the clavier, the lute, and gave him lessons in composition and singing. In all of these the boy excelled. While he was still a child, he performed throughout Italy, and his voice was widely acclaimed everywhere. People wrote that he sang like an angel, and some people called him "the divine."

By the time he was twenty years old, Frescobaldi had performed in all the principal cities of Italy. Everyone admired both his organ playing and his singing, and many people followed him from city to city just to hear him.

At twenty-one he was accepted as a singer and organist at the Congregation and Academy of Masters and Professors of Rome. This was an exceptional honor for one so young, because only the very best and most accomplished musicians were accepted.

But more important than the honors he received was the fact that Frescobaldi understood music and felt it deeply. His training had prepared him not only to keep abreast of all the exciting things that were happening in music, but also to add something of his own. And it soon became apparent that the instruments he most enjoyed were the organ and harpsichord. It was for these instruments he hoped to compose.

In the meantime, since composers did not generally make very much money and had to pay to have their pieces published, he needed work. And he needed work of a permanent kind, something that did not require his traveling around all the time, as his concert schedule did.

In January of 1607, he was appointed organist of the St. John of Latran Church in Rome. This was the beginning of his professional career as an organist. However, he kept this position only three months, for the salary was not a good one; and when a better position with a better salary was offered, he took it. His new job was as leader of a group of musicians who were to entertain the Pope's envoy to Brussels.

In the spring of 1608, Frescobaldi and the other musicians of the party went to Brussels. The envoy they were to serve, Bentivoglia, loved music, and the situation was a happy one, except that Frescobaldi did not have an organ to play. He sang and played on the lute and led the other musicians in concerts. He composed madrigals and even published a book of them. But there was something missing and he knew it. He longed to be working on things that seemed more important to him.

After one year in Brussels, Frescobaldi returned to Rome. A contest was going to be held to select a new organist for St. Peter's. This position was the most sought after in all Italy, and Frescobaldi wanted to take part in the contest. Here was the kind of work he wanted.

He arrived in Rome sometime before the contest was to take place, and in preparation he practiced almost constantly. Few men of his day could work as hard as he could work or could perform as steadily. Perhaps his excellent training as a boy and his early rounds of performances had given him this enormous endurance. But whatever the reason, when the day of the contest came, he was well prepared and he played more brilliantly than any of the other contestants. So he was the one chosen for the job.

Frescobaldi had been given the most important position he could ever hope to have at the age of twenty-six. It was a most unusual honor, and he began working at once to make the most of it. The job itself did not actually begin for several months, so he had time to prepare. He practiced the organ many hours a day, and the rest of his time he spent composing the kind of music he really wanted to write—serious works for the organ and harpsichord. Among these were toccatas, ricercari and canzoni. Toccatas are intricate and difficult pieces of music that show off both the performer and the composer. Frescobaldi's toccatas are among the finest that have ever been written. Ricercari and canzoni were early forms of the fugue, complex patterns of melody with great depth and richness. His were unlike any that had ever been heard before in beauty, complexity and harmony.

Frescobaldi was already well known because of his performances as a boy. So when his new position was announced and people became aware of the preparations he was making, they were anxious to hear him play. The first time he played in St. Peter's, thirty thousand people thronged the church.

More and more new ideas came from him. He began to experiment with harmony. During the Baroque Period the bass accompaniment of a composition was known as the "Basso Continuo." This was a continuous bass written in a system of musical shorthand. The composer put down the notes with numbers above or below them. These numbers indicated the chords that were to be played. For example, if the numbers were $\frac{5}{3}$ the upper note of the chord was a fifth, or five notes, up from the bass note and the lower one was a third or three notes, up. Frescobaldi used chords in his accompaniments that had never been used before. With them he made unusual modulations. When a composer introduces modulations, he is changing the key in which the piece is written. For example, he may begin a piece in C major, modulate to F major and then return to the original key. This is generally accomplished by a skillful use of chords, but no one had ever done it so well before.

Not too long after he started work at St. Peter's, some of Frescobaldi's compositions were gathered together and published in a volume called *Fiori Musicali* (*Musical Flowers*). Each of the toccatas, ricercari and canzoni in this collection is a masterpiece.

But though Frescobaldi attracted huge crowds to St. Peter's and though his fame spread throughout Italy, his salary was small and remained small. This was upsetting to Frescobaldi because he wanted to be married. Finally he gave up waiting for an increase in salary and married his fiancée, Orsolo Travaglini. The marriage took place on February 12, 1613.

A few months after the marriage, the Duke of Mantua came to Frescobaldi and offered him a position in his court at a higher salary. As a further inducement the Duke promised to help Frescobaldi get some of his compositions published. The offer sounded attractive, but Frescobaldi was not sure he could trust the Duke. This was the Duke who had recently dismissed Monteverdi for no reason at all. So Frescobaldi accepted the offer, but left his wife in Rome until he was sure things would work out well in Mantua.

His decision to leave his wife behind was a wise one, for the Duke did not keep any of his promises. And to make matters worse, Frescobaldi was not well treated at court. He was looked down upon and ignored. After only two months he left Mantua and returned to Rome.

Back in Rome, he resumed his position at St. Peter's. There his financial situation improved somewhat because between 1615 and 1628 ten different volumes of his works were published. All the expenses of publication were paid for by some of his admirers. But by 1628, he and his wife had five children, and they needed more money than they had. Once again Frescobaldi was willing to consider a new job if it offered him the salary he needed to support his family. And such an offer came from Ferdinand II, Grand Duke of Tuscany. The job would be in Florence, where he would be a court musician.

Frescobaldi's life as a court musician was a busy one. He was organist, harpsichordist and composer for the court. This was good, because Frescobaldi liked to be busy. But composing had come to be the most important part of music for him, and at the court he was not free to do as he wished. The Duke ordered him to compose only "light music" for the entertainment of the court. Instead of toccatas, ricercari and canzoni, he wrote several volumes of light airs. This seemed a waste of time and talent to him. He wanted to use himself to the full.

So finally in 1634 Frescobaldi and his family returned to Rome. There he was able to resume his old job at St. Peter's. Everyone welcomed him with joy. And he in turn was delighted to be able once again to play and compose the kind of music he loved.

To make the situation even better, he was given an increase in salary and was also given the job of repairing the organs in St. Peter's, which increased his income further. To favor Frescobaldi still more, his favorite son, Domenico, was given the position of a clerk at the Vatican. The puzzling thing about this was that although Frescobaldi was considered to be a great musician and was highly thought of, Domenico earned more money as a clerk than his father did as organist and composer of St. Peter's.

In order to meet expenses, Frescobaldi accepted pupils who came and lived with his family. In this way he not only received money for lessons, but also for room and board.

His reputation spread all over Europe. Among his pupils was the gifted Viennese composer, Johann Jacob Froberger, who was sent to Rome for study by the Emperor Ferdinand II of Austria. Froberger studied with Frescobaldi for three and a half years.

When Froberger returned to Austria as court organist, he was full of praise for his teacher. He did all he could to make Frescobaldi's works known in Austria and Germany. It was because of him that Johann Sebastian Bach came to know Frescobaldi's music. He was much impressed, especially by the *Musical Flowers* and used themes he found there in some of his own compositions.

But though his fame spread, Frescobaldi did not rely on past accomplishments to maintain his reputation. All his life he continued to have new ideas and to put them to work. He was continually building on what he had done before and on the things he learned from other people. His mind always seemed to be ahead of his fingers and his pen. He was a positive genius at improvising, that is making up music on the spur of the moment. A writer of the period told of one instance when Frescobaldi did an especially fine piece of improvising:

> One day Frescobaldi did a startling thing. He had just finished a solemn piece of sacred music. After a short pause he broke into a simple tune. His listeners looked up in surprise. In that simple tune they recognized *Berga-masca,* an old peasant tune. To their astonishment, it grew into a maze of sound, now slow, now fast, in one rhythm, now in another. But

the tune of the peasant dance rang clear throughout the performance.

In his later years he invented a new kind of canzona. Originally a stylized kind of folk song, the canzona had been a rather simple kind of vocal or instrumental composition up to his time. But he gave it a complexity that made it a kind of fugue.

He toyed with tempo and introduced the word "rubato," which means robbed. By it he meant to steal a little from the tempo by playing some phrases faster, but to give back what was stolen by playing the next phrases slower.

It was also Frescobaldi who first experimented with the "Well-Tempered System of Tuning." This meant that he composed music in all the major and minor keys. It was the same idea that Bach later used in his forty-eight preludes and fugues, known as *The Well-Tempered Clavichord*.

Few musicians of his day could keep up with all of the new ideas Frescobaldi introduced. To help them and to make sure his music was played as he wanted it played, he wrote an introduction or preface to each composition. In these he explained just how he wanted the music performed. And today by reading these, we, too, can know just how he wanted his pieces to sound.

Frescobaldi's life came to an end quite suddenly. He was stricken with a severe fever in February of 1643 and after ten days of illness, died. He was sixty years old.

The best musicians in Rome sang his funeral mass and on his gravestone were the words, "The most famous organist of his time."

But he is remembered not just as a famous organist.

He is far more famed today as the first great Italian composer of music for the organ and the harpsichord. He was a prodigious performer, but we, of course, can never hear him play. It is his sensitive compositions that we know and remember him by, the work of a man who obviously knew music well and was not afraid to try new things.

Some of his works have since been arranged for instruments other than the ones they were originally written for. The harpsichord pieces, for example, have been rewritten for piano. One of the organ toccatas was first arranged as a cello solo and then as a piece for two pianos. Some of the pieces for the harpsichord are even played on the guitar. But old instruments sometimes return, and recently a canzona of Frescobaldi was performed using the recorder, harpsichord, viola da gamba and krummhorn.

Arcangelo Corelli

1653-1713

TO SOME PEOPLE A LOVE OF MUSIC COMES EARLY AND grows until nothing else is ever so important. This was true of Arcangelo Corelli. Music first became important to him when he heard a priest from a neighboring town play the violin. Although Corelli was still a small boy at the time, he wept for joy at the sound.

The Corelli family did not live in a great center of culture and learning. Their small village, Fusignani, was midway between the cities of Bologna and Ravenna, both musical centers; but Fusignani, itself, did not have many musicians.

After he heard the priest play, young Corelli pleaded with his mother for lessons on the violin. But the only teacher available was the priest, himself, and he lived two miles away in the town of Saint Savino.

The Corellis were wealthy, although Signor Corelli

had died before Arcangelo was born. There was no question of not being able to afford the lessons or the violin. The problem was the distance between the two towns. In those days the only way for a boy to go back and forth was to walk. But Arcangelo did not mind, and so the lessons began. He walked back and forth each day regardless of the weather, happy because he had the one thing he wanted in all the world.

Sometimes it was so hot that on his way home he had to stop and rest under a tree. Very often, while he was resting, he would take his violin out of its case and play. The sounds spread over the neighborhood and people gathered to listen. Even after only a few lessons, his playing was worth listening to.

Because he learned so quickly, a new problem arose before too many years had passed. Arcangelo had become a better violinist than his teacher. There were no other teachers near so his only opportunity for further learning lay in Bologna or Ravenna. Each was about seventy-five miles away. Of the two Bologna was the greater musical center. So Arcangelo's mother decided that that was where he must go. He was thirteen years old when he left his home and his family to further his knowledge of music.

In Bologna, Corelli studied violin, organ and harpsichord, as well as theory of music. He made unusual progress in all of his studies. When he was just seventeen he was accepted at the Philharmonia Academy in Bologna. Most students accepted there were older.

At the Academy, Corelli studied with Giovanni Benvenuti, who had founded the first school for the training of violinists. Corelli studied with Benvenuti for four years, and at the end of that time he was a truly remarkable violinist.

The place to go next, Corelli decided was Rome. In those days Rome was the place for those who wanted to do important things. Everything there was done in a grand style. And music was especially important in everything that happened. For festive occasions the music was written in a style called Colossal Baroque. Huge choral works were written for many singers accompanied by viols, trombones, trumpets, cornetts, and organs. For a boy who wanted to become an important violinist, to whom music was all important, Rome was the place to go. And so, in 1671 Corelli went.

It was even more exciting than he had expected. The music was so grand that he not only wanted to play it, he wanted to compose some of it himself. To learn composition, he began to study with the finest teacher in Rome, Matteo Simonelli.

Simonelli taught Corelli much about the writing of music. In later years, when Corelli became well known, Simonelli was proud to have it said that Corelli was his most celebrated pupil.

Corelli finished his studies with Simonelli in 1673. Where he went from there is not known. Undoubtedly he spent his time practicing the violin and composing. Then in the beginning of 1675 he became violinist in the Church of St. Louis of France in Rome.

By this time he was a violinist to astonish any audience. He played double and triple stops, which means two and three notes at one time, instead of one as everyone else had always done. His scales and arpeggios were faster and better than those of any other violinist. He made the violin sing like a human voice, people said.

Corelli himself was excited by the sounds his violin made. When he played, those who saw him said, "His face became distorted, his eyes became red as fire, and his eyeballs rolled as if in agony."

Although Corelli's technique was undoubtedly ex-
quisite, his playing may have been helped by the violin
he played. The instrument, itself, had just been perfected. It was the time of Antonio Stradivari, the great
violin maker of Cremona, and he had made the instrument Corelli played.

VIOLIN

During the years Corelli was performing so mar-
velously, he was also composing. In 1681 his first set
of trio sonatas was published. The sonatas were written in three parts but were meant to be played by four
instruments. Two violins performed the upper part, the

'cello played the bass part, and the harpsichord played the accompaniment.

Corelli dedicated these first works to Queen Christina of Sweden, who lived in Rome and was an important patroness of music. His dedication said, "If your Majesty would be so good as to accept and protect these first fruits of my studies, and I hope she will, I will be encouraged to continue other works already sketched."

Queen Christina was so impressed she invited him to perform his works at one of her musical evenings. This was a mark of distinction because only the most important musicians played for her.

The sonatas were duly performed at one of the Queen's musical affairs, and almost immediately became popular not only in Rome but in cities everywhere. They reached as far as England in a remarkably short time. The composer Henry Purcell received a copy from a friend traveling in Italy and was so impressed that he used them for models when he wrote his own trio sonatas.

Musicians came from all over to meet Corelli and talk with him. To them all, he conveyed his fine sense of the importance of music and his dedication to his work.

One of those who came was a musician named Strungk, from Hanover, Germany.

"What is your instrument?" asked Corelli the first time they met.

"I can play," answered Strungk, "upon the harpsichord and a little on the violin, and should esteem myself extremely happy if I could hear you perform on this latter instrument."

Corelli very politely agreed to this request. He

played a solo, and Strungk accompanied on the harpsichord. Afterward Strungk played a toccata, and Corelli was much impressed with the man's ability. Then Strungk took up the violin and on a pretense of tuning it, lowered the *A* string to a *G*. When he played, the music sounded dissonant and unpleasant.

Corelli cried out in broken German, "I am called Arcangelo, a name that in the language of my country means arc-angel. But let me tell you, sir, you are an arch-devil."

Strungk laughed and so did Corelli, and the two became good friends. When Strungk left Rome for Hamburg, he carried with him a copy of Corelli's trio sonatas.

Corelli's next set of trio sonatas were published in Bologna in 1685. At the time of publication they had not yet been performed, and a group of players was soon chosen to give the first performance. When the players were rehearsing for the first time, they came to a certain part that puzzled them. They stopped and looked at each other in surprise. The work was full of fifths—notes that are five tones apart on a scale, such as *C* and *G* or *D* and *A*. And furthermore, there were a number of consecutive fifths, one following another. This broke all the rules of harmony. One of the musicians wrote to Corelli and asked why he had made such an awful mistake. Corelli replied that he had made no mistake at all. He had wanted to write the measures just as they were written. Eleven letters passed between the musician and Corelli, but he would not change the measures. What he had done was daring, would be daring even today. But Corelli did not care. It was the music that was important to him. And if it required daring to write as he wished, then he was more than willing to be daring.

This episode, which became known as the "episode of the fifths" did not make Corelli less popular. It just served to make him more prominent. And in the summer of 1687 he was asked by Cardinal Panfili to be his music master. Cardinal Panfili was then one of the most important patrons of music in Rome. Corelli, his servants, and his favorite pupil, Matteo Fornari, went to live in the Panfili Palace.

As the conductor of Panfili's orchestra, Corelli participated in many musical events in the city. He performed in the squares of the city, in the Panfili Palace, in other palaces, and also for Queen Christina. Many of the performances were long and elaborate. One, for example, consisted of a cantata in the Colossal Baroque style. It was composed for a special occasion by Corelli's friend, Pasquini. The work called for five vocal soloists, a chorus of one hundred, and an orchestra of one hundred and fifty.

Corelli kept his position with Panfili until 1691. In that year Cardinal Panfili moved to Bologna, and Corelli became the head of the musicians in the court of Cardinal Pietro Ottoboni in Rome. Ottoboni was a nephew of Pope Alessandro VIII, and like Cardinal Panfili, loved music.

Corelli had a fine apartment in the palace of the Cardinal and in addition received a fine salary. Most important, Ottoboni treated Corelli not as a servant, but as an equal. The two men were great friends.

Corelli did not let even the Cardinal offend his sense of the importance of music. For Corelli music always came first. Once he was playing one of his own compositions before a small group of people in the private apartments of the Cardinal. At the height of the piece, the Cardinal began talking to one of the men present. At once Corelli stopped his music and lay down his instrument. The Cardinal, surprised at the interruption, asked if a string was broken.

"No," answered Corelli, "I was only afraid I was interrupting your business."

The Cardinal, who knew a fine musician could only play his best before an appreciative audience, broke off the conversation and asked to hear the entire composition again.

It was important to Corelli not only that the Cardinal and his friends hear good music, but that others also have such an opportunity. The Cardinal felt just as Corelli did. So Corelli arranged a series of weekly concerts, given in the chapel of the church adjoining the palace. These concerts, known as "the Mondays at Ottoboni's", were among the most important musical events of the time in Rome. Corelli played his violin, and the Cardinal's orchestra performed works of all composers. People came from all over Rome, and all over Europe, to hear the music.

Playing for the Cardinal and planning the Monday concerts all took time. But still Corelli managed to be head of the musicians of the congregation of St. Cecilia, one of the most important churches of Rome, and to continue to compose music. There was time for anything that had to do with music.

In 1700 his compositions for solo violin were published. These were the first solo sonatas for violin ever written. They were written so perfectly that they were used as models by other composers of the Baroque Period. The last sonata of the set, became the most popular. It consisted of twenty-three variations on a famous melody called "La Follia."

Corelli was often invited to other cities to perform his works, but he was happy with his work in Rome, and he hated to waste time in travel. However, the King of Naples was so persistent in his invitations that finally in 1708 Corelli consented to visit him.

Corelli took several of his own musicians with him to Naples to make sure that his works would be well played. When he arrived, however, he discovered that his precaution was not at all necessary. The orchestra in Naples played well at the very first rehearsal.

To his own musicians Corelli cried out, "My, they play well in Naples." This pleased the men in the orchestra who worked even harder to do what he wanted. As a result, Corelli's compositions were shown off to a great advantage and he was a grand success.

Not all of his experiences in Naples were equally pleasant, however. At his palace the King asked Corelli to perform a violin sonata. Apparently one of the slow movements was too long for the King, because he walked out. Corelli was furious, but there was nothing he could do. He could not speak to the King of Naples as he did to Cardinal Ottoboni. The King obviously did not understand the importance of music.

Another time, the King asked Corelli to play one of Alessandro Scarlatti's compositions for violin. Scarlatti was the head of all the music in Naples at that time. The part for the leading violinists seems to have been poorly noted down. Although Corelli tried hard, he could not read the music and kept playing the wrong notes. Finally Scarlatti, himself, who was present, called out the right notes. This humiliated Corelli so much that he walked off the stage and went back to Rome immediately. It was important to him to be in a place where his work was appreciated.

Back in Rome, Corelli spent less and less time in the fancy apartment in the palace of Cardinal Ottoboni and more and more time in his own small apartment outside the palace. He had this apartment for his personal and precious possessions. Next to music, his greatest love was painting, and he kept his very fine collection in his own apartment. More important, however, was the privacy he found there to compose. For as time went on, it was composing and not performing that held his interest.

The most popular musical form of the Baroque Period was the concerto grosso. It was usually written in four movements for several solo instruments and an orchestra. The part for solo instruments was called the "concertina" and the part for the full orchestra was the "tutti." Although many composers of the Baroque Period wrote concerti grossi, it was Corelli who did most with them.

Corelli's works were written in five or more movements instead of the usual four, and they presented more variety and contrast between the movements and between the solo parts and the parts for the entire orchestra than those that had been written before.

There is no doubt that Corelli's concerti grossi prepared the way for those written by Bach and Handel. Bach used one of Corelli's themes as the subject for an organ fugue, called "The Corelli Fugue." Handel, who met Corelli at one of the Mondays at Ottoboni's copied out many of Corelli's works note by note.

Corelli's sonatas, too, added much that was new to the world of music. They were written in four movements: slow, fast, slow, fast. This pattern was followed until the time of Joseph Haydn, and even after.

In France the Baroque Composer, François Couperin heard Corelli's sonatas and loved them. When Couperin composed his first sonatas, he wrote an introduction to them that he called "A Composer's Confession to his Public." In this he said, "The first sonata of this set was the first that I composed and the first to be composed in France. Delighted with those of Signor Corelli, whose works I shall love as long as I live, I made so bold as to compose one similar."

Corelli died when he was fifty-seven years old, on January 6, 1713. He left everything he had to Cardinal Ottoboni. The Cardinal kept only the collection of paintings and gave the money Corelli had saved and the furnishings of his apartment to his relatives. To Corelli's favorite pupil, Fornari, the Cardinal gave Corelli's beautiful Stradivari violin and his other instruments.

Some years before Corelli had been made a member of the Academy of Arcadians, a select group of nobles and poets. At that time he had been given the Greek name, Arcomelo, "leader of singing," by the society. And it is as a leader of singing that he is still remembered. Although he is the only composer of the Baroque Period who did not write compositions for the voice, his great skill make the violin sing. His dedication to music as an end in itself and his pioneer efforts to create fine music for the violin and other stringed instruments made people aware of the capacities of these instruments. His singing melodies for them are still heard the world over.

Antonio Vivaldi

1678-1741

IN THE EARLY EIGHTEENTH CENTURY IN VENICE, ONE of the places to go on a Sunday or a holiday for entertainment was The Pietà, or the Ospedale della Pietà, as it was more formally called. This was a home for girls and young women where, next to religious studies, music was the most important subject. All of the girls learned to sing and to play instruments. Concerts were held every Sunday and every holiday, and people came from all over Europe to hear the performances.

The girls sang; they played the violin, flute, horn, oboe, organ, 'cello, double-bass and bassoon. No instrument was large enough to frighten them. And the lovely music that came from them, visitors reported, was heard nowhere else in all Italy. Many who went to hear the girls found it especially charming to see delicate white hands playing a large double-bass or a pair of young and rosy cheeks puffing with all their might at a horn. And sometimes a young and pretty nun in a white robe with a bouquet of pomegranate flowers in her hair conducted the orchestra.

Even royalty occasionally visited the school. When this happened the day was more festive than ever. The canal in the vicinity of the Pietà was lighted with special lights, gold brocades were hung in the auditorium, the candles in the crystal chandeliers were lighted, and everything glittered and sparkled.

The head of all of this at the time was a young priest named Antonio Vivaldi. He had been born in Venice, had grown up there, and had studied the violin, organ, and music theory there. His father had been a violinist in the chapel of St. Mark's Cathedral.

Although Vivaldi's great interest as a boy was in music, he was persuaded, perhaps by one of his music teachers, to become a priest. Such a decision was not too unusual because at that time priests were interested in many things outside of the Church and often had varied responsibilities. Vivaldi had therefore received his Minor Orders for the priesthood in 1696 when he was eighteen, and his Final Orders on March 23, 1703, at the age of twenty-five.

As a priest, Vivaldi's interest in music did not diminish. In fact, the story was told that soon after he received his Final Orders he was saying Mass one day when an idea for a fugue came to him. Not wanting to lose the idea, he left the altar to jot the idea down and then came back and finished the Mass. The incident was said to have been reported to the authorities of the Church, who forbade him to say Mass in public again. Although this tale was widespread during his life, Vivaldi himself denied it, saying that he did not say Mass in public out of choice, because his ill health and especially his asthma made it difficult for him to do so.

Whatever the truth of the matter was, it is known that his health was poor and that he did not have a church as his responsibility, but soon after his ordination was placed in charge of the Ospedale della Pietà.

BASSOON

Here he was supposed to supervise the running of the institution, but his most important task was to organize the musical training of the girls, teaching them to play the violin, conducting the orchestra, purchasing instruments and composing works for the girls to play.

The Pietà under Vivaldi's leadership must have been a pleasant place and the music lessons must have been enjoyable, for the girls seem not to have ever tired of playing and rehearsing. In order to satisfy their musical hunger, Vivaldi wrote vast amounts of music. And as he worked, he developed a new form of concerto. A concerto is an orchestral piece that features a solo performer. Vivaldi wrote concertos for violin, viola d'amore, 'cello, flute, oboe, trumpet and even mandolin and bassoon. He was the first composer ever to write a concerto for a bassoon, and he did not stop with one. He wrote thirty-seven.

The new form that Vivaldi created consisted of three movements. The first movement was always quick, the second slow, and the third quick again. The slow movements were his unique contribution because, until his time, the slow movements of a concerto merely linked the two fast ones. His were instead beautiful singing movements, complete in themselves. Also, most of his concertos have a brilliant cadenza at the end of the first movement. These give the solo performer a special chance to show off his ability.

Perhaps because Vivaldi was writing for young people, or perhaps just because he liked new effects and had a sense of gaiety about him, he wrote music imitating the sounds of birds. He wrote a concerto for violin called "The Cuckoo Concerto" imitating the sound of a cuckoo. In a flute concerto called "The Goldfinch" he not only made the flute imitate the song of the goldfinch, but also had the string instruments accompanying the flute give the effect of the peck, peck, peck of the goldfinch's beak when he is hunting for his breakfast.

Some people poked fun at what they called "Vivaldi's farmyard music," but in spite of what was said, these concertos became popular almost immediately.

Closely akin to the farmyard music, was Vivaldi's initiation of what came to be called "program music."

That is, music inspired by a special story or poem and expressing the ideas of the story or poem in the music. No one had ever thought of doing this before him for anything but a vocal composition.

One of Vivaldi's pieces of program music was a set of four violin concertos called "The Seasons." There was one concerto for each of the four seasons and a poem telling what the music was intended to express appeared at the beginning of each. These read in part:

SPRING

Spring has come and the birds greet it with happy songs. And at the same time the streams run softly murmuring to the breathing of the gentle breezes.

SUMMER

In the season made harsh by the burning sun, men and the herds languish . . . the cuckoo unlocks his voice and soon the songs of the turtle-dove and the goldfinch are heard.

FALL

With songs and dances the peasants celebrate the happiness of the fine harvest.

WINTER

To tremble frozen in the icy snow, to have excessive cold set one's teeth to chattering . . .

When one listens to Vivaldi's descriptive music of the seasons, one can easily feel the cold of winter as well as hear the peasants stamping their feet and dancing with joy because of the fine harvest.

Vivaldi also composed operas. Some of these were

for performance in the Pietà, but not all. Some were for opera houses outside of Venice. They were very popular and Vivaldi had many requests to write more of them. It was difficult, however, for him to find time to write them when he was busy with his duties at the Pietà.

In 1713 the directors of the Pietà granted Vivaldi a leave so he might have time to compose more operas. When he had even a little time, he was able to write prodigiously. He could dash off three operas in less than three months. And with his opera *Tito Manlio* he set something of a record even for him. On the title page of this opera is written *Musica di Vivaldi fatto in 5 Giorni*—"Music of Vivaldi made in five days."

And it was not only operas that Vivaldi could compose quickly. He prided himself on being able to write a concerto faster than a copyist could copy it. An example of his speed was once given by a German musician traveling in Venice. He was anxious to meet Vivaldi and sent his servant to him requesting an appointment. This account of what took place shows just how fast Vivaldi could compose:

> On Wednesday, March 6, 1715, Vivaldi, the famous composer and violinist, came to my house. I spoke of some concerti grossi that I would like to have from him. In the afternoon of March 9, Vivaldi came to me and brought ten concerti grossi which he said he had composed for me. Imagine in three days! Not only did Vivaldi sell these to me, but he came from time to time to teach them to me.

Though Vivaldi's main work was at the Pietà, for many years when he had time he did many other things. He composed, of course, but he was also in great demand as a solo violinist. Those who saw him perform his concertos never forgot either him or his music. It was an exciting thing to see the frail Vivaldi with his long disheveled red hair, dressed in his priest's robe, tossing off the brilliant candenza to one of his concertos. Violinists came from England, Austria, and Holland to listen to him play as well as to study with him.

Since Vivaldi was a sickly man, it is especially amazing to realize how much he accomplished. His busy schedule of teaching, composing, and performing in Venice was not enough for him. He sometimes even accepted invitations to play or conduct in other countries. He became famous all over Europe.

Wherever Vivaldi went or whatever he did, however, he always came back to the Pietà. There the girls performed his works at every one of their concerts. And in 1738 the King of Bavaria made a special trip to Venice just to hear one of these performances. On that occasion "The Red Priest," as Vivaldi was often called because of his red hair, was showered with honors and with presents. It seemed as if he had reached the height of his career.

Immediately after this performance Vivaldi went away, and this time he did not return. He completely disappeared. No one heard of him again, and his works were no longer played in Venice. Although he had been the most important composer in Venice for forty years, it was almost as if he had never existed.

For years those who were curious about his disappearance thought Vivaldi had gone to Vienna. But no one was able to prove this until two hundred years later. In 1938 information was found indicating that he did indeed go to Vienna and that he died there on

July 17, 1741, a poor and neglected man. Like Mozart fifty years later, he was buried in a pauper's grave.

His music did not disappear with him, fortunately. It was not played in Venice, but it lived on in some places. Johann Sebastian Bach, for example, said that he learned everything he knew about the concerto from Vivaldi. Bach never met Vivaldi, but he studied his works and used them as models. Bach also arranged some of Vivaldi's violin concertos for other instruments, sixteen of them for harpsichord, one for four harpsichords with string accompaniment, and four for organ.

Even Beethoven may have been influenced by Vivaldi. His Pastoral Symphony is about nature and in some ways recalls Vivaldi's set of violin concertos about the seasons.

But although Vivaldi's works were important to other musicians, for a long period of time they were seldom performed and most were lost or forgotten. Only in recent years have they been rediscovered and published by an Italian publisher, Ricordi. Altogether, Vivaldi composed 447 solo concerts and concerti grossi, 44 operas, 28 secular cantatas and several oratorios. At least, that many have been found and published. New works are constantly being added to those already known.

In 1965 the first performance in the United States of Vivaldi's *The Gloria Mass* took place. This beautiful work has since been compared to the great *St. Matthew Passion* of Bach. And so, once again, Vivaldi is recognized as the genius he was. But perhaps he comes into his own most when his works are enjoyed by children and young people. For it was for the girls of the Pietà that many of his most inventive things were written.

Jean Baptiste Lully

1632-1687

IT WAS CARNIVAL TIME IN FLORENCE, AND RICH AND poor mingled together in the gay carnival grounds. Among the poor was Gianbattista Lulli, the son of a miller, who had run away from his chores at the mill to join the strolling musicians. Young Lulli played the guitar and was never so happy as when he could strum his instrument and sing gay songs.

Among the wealthy at the carnival was the Duke of Guise, a French nobleman living in Florence. He could not help but notice the attractive young boy playing with the musicians. He seemed highly talented. So the Duke stopped to talk to him. In the conversation the Duke mentioned his cousin, the Duchess of Montpensier, who lived in Paris and was looking for a boy to help in the kitchen and to speak Italian with her. The Duchess loved music and had many musical performances at her house, the Duke went on to say. Would Lulli, perhaps, be interested in going to Paris?

Lulli was excited. Life at the mill was pleasant. There was singing there and sometimes there was even a little money for guitar lessons. There was time for practicing and making up little tunes on the guitar. But

GUITAR

this was not all that Gianbattista wanted. The world was a big place, and he wanted to see more of it than he did at the mill. He did not want to be a miller all his life.

The boy hurried home and told his parents about the opportunity offered to him. There were other children in the Lulli family, many mouths to feed and many bodies to clothe on a limited income. Although the family did not want to send their son away, it seemed too good an opportunity to miss. Therefore, young Lulli was given permission to accept the position, and in a few days he was off to Paris and what he hoped would be a merry life of his own.

At the home of the Duchess of Montpensier, Lulli, who soon changed the spelling of his name to Jean Baptiste Lully, in the French manner, helped in the kitchen, spoke Italian with his mistress, and in his leisure, played the guitar and sang. He worked harder at his music than ever before, because the lovely music he heard coming from the performances in the salon made him determined to become a musician.

The guitar was not enough to know. This was apparent. Fine musicians did not play the guitar at salon performances. So he borrowed a violin and taught himself to play it. And once he learned, he began composing airs for it, which the Duchess heard him playing.

She realized that her kitchen boy and Italian conversationalist was a gifted musician. When she learned that he had taught himself the violin, she arranged for him to have lessons with a fine teacher. In a short time he had learned to play well. She also allowed him to listen more closely to the concerts and watch the ballets that were given in her salon. Of all this, Lully took full advantage. He wanted to learn as much as he could in whatever way he could.

To be ambitious however, did not also mean that he could not be mischievous. And one day he wrote a sarcastic poem about the Duchess and set it to music. Somehow, this bit of work came to the attention of the Duchess, who dismissed Lully immediately.

Lully had been in the employ of the Duchess for five years. He was now nineteen and for the first time he was on his own in Paris. What was he to do? He felt certain that no one else would give him the opportunities the Duchess had, and yet he was determined to make his way and succeed.

The King of France at that time was young, younger than Lully; in fact, Louis XIV was only fifteen years old. Like other kings and nobles of his time, however, he was much interested in music, and although he was young, he was an excellent musician. He always had music around him, and had organized a famous band, the Twenty-Four Violins.

Somehow the King heard of Lully and also of Lully's problem. Perhaps he even heard Lully's song about the Duchess and agreed with it. Whatever it was he heard, it made him send for Lully and ask him to be one of the Twenty-Four Violins.

In the palace of the King, Lully's cleverness was appreciated, as it had never been in the palace of the Duchess. And his age was a great help, undoubtedly. A boy of nineteen was much more pleasant company for a king of fifteen than the older courtiers and musicians that surrounded him. So Louis XIV watched Lully with interest. Because the King was a fine dancer himself, he saw to it that Lully learned to dance. Ballet was important at the court, and to take part in court entertainments one had to know how to dance.

Only three months after Lully came to the court of the King, he danced beside the King in the "Ballet of the Night," a popular work at the time. Lully's performance was all the King could have asked. And the King himself was a brilliant success. In fact, some people now think that the ballet gave the King the nickname he is still known by, "the Sun King"; for in the ballet he wore a dazzling costume. It had a symbol of the sun across the chest and a crown of sunbeams shining from the neck, shoulders, and wrists.

As time went on, Lully learned more and more to please the King, and the King became Lully's greatest admirer. Lully danced gracefully, he played the violin well, and he composed charming minuets. One of these became the official dance of the court.

As Lully came to know the King better, he could get almost anything he wanted. Flattery, for example, worked wonders when he wanted a special favor. And eventually, he was so skillful he convinced the King that it would improve the music of the court if he organized his own group of violinists. This group, composed of sixteen violinists, was known as the Little Violins. Soon there was great rivalry between Lully's group and the old Twenty-Four Violins, but Lully was so effective that his group rapidly became the most important.

To achieve is one thing, to make something of that achievement is another. Lully did not rest content with getting what he wanted. He worked to do what he had promised. At rehearsals of the Little Violins, he was very strict. He let no mistake or shoddy playing go by. His players must play as one and not as sixteen. If a violinist played a wrong note, he would get into such a rage that he would break the violin on the player's back. But in a few moments he would feel sorry for what he had done and pay the violinist three times the value of the violin and perhaps even take the man to dinner.

In addition to conducting his men, Lully composed music for them. And here he was not content with the "good enough" either. He wanted to do more than write charming minuets. So he arranged to have lessons both on the harpsichord and in composition with the best teachers in Paris. In a short time he was able to write highly interesting compositions for the Little Violins, and he also began to write music for ballets.

The ballets used at the French court had always been minuets. But Lully decided that this was foolish. There were other dance forms that would lend interest and variety to the entertainments. So he used gavottes, bourrées, and passepieds in his lively dances. Some people said that Lully had turned dancing into buffoonery. But the King enjoyed the lively music and the dancing that went with it, and that was most important to Lully.

By the time Lully was twenty-nine, his position at court was so solid, his reputation so well established, that no festivity was complete without his music. He knew that his future was assured and that his life would be spent in France; so he became a citizen. He had now lived in France longer than he had lived in Italy.

At about the same time, he married. His wife was Madeleine Lambert, whose father was also a court musician. The King was so pleased with the match that he himself signed the marriage contract, and at the same time promoted Lully to Master of the Music of the Royal Family, a position that carried a fine salary with it.

It was later that same year that Lully first met Molière. Molière was at that time the finest playwright in France. Together Lully and Molière produced what they called comic ballets. These were stories written by Molière and set to music by Lully. One of them, the *Bourgeois Gentilhomme,* Lully not only prepared the music for, but also acted in. He took the part of a valet disguised as a Turkish nobleman. His performance was so amusing that he received more applause than anyone else. The comic ballet became one of the King's favorite kinds of entertainment.

In another of Molière's plays, *Monsieur Pourceaugnac,* Lully played the part of a doctor using a false name. At the first performance, Lully looked down from the stage at the audience and noticed that the King did not seem to be enjoying himself. Disappointed and determined to please the King, Lully jumped down from the stage onto the harpsichord in the orchestra and with a tremendous clatter smashed the instrument into bits. The King roared with laughter.

But these bits of acting and clowning were only one side of Lully, the side that kept him a favorite at court and made it possible for him to do the thing he really wanted to do, which was to compose music.

Lully was the first French composer to experiment with opera. And for the French court, he knew a different form was wanted from the form of the Italian operas. He replaced the long elaborate arias with many short songs in a graceful minuet rhythm. He used larger choruses, and was able to have mass scenes that added to the spectacle. To please the King, he put ballets into his works.

From the first note on, a Lully opera was different from earlier operas. Even his overtures were different. Before Lully, overtures were merely short pieces of music designed to quiet the audience. But Lully used the overture to set the mood for the entire opera. Most of his overtures were written in three parts. The first consisted of slow majestic chords, and probably signaled the entrance of the King into the Royal Box. The second part was written in a quick dancelike rhythm. The third was slow and quiet, to soothe the ear for the enjoyment of the opera. This form of overture became known as the "Lullian Overture" and was imitated all over Europe.

Lully worked hard when he was composing an opera. If an idea came into his head in the middle of the night, he got up and went to his harpsichord and played and sang until he was sure that he had done with it what he wanted. It took him about three months of constant work to finish an opera, and even when it was ready to be rehearsed, he continued to pour his energies into it. He worked not only with the orchestra but also with the singers and the dancers on every note and every movement.

Lully's operas were so popular that the arias and songs were played everywhere. Cooks sang them as they stirred their stews and cleaning women hummed the tunes as they swept the floors. Once as Lully was riding in his carriage, he heard a group of street musicians playing tunes from his operas, and he stopped the carriage to show the violinists just how the music should be played.

On days when his operas were being performed, the streets approaching the new opera house in Paris, built especially for Lully, were filled with long lines of carriages. Some people walked miles and miles to hear a performance. Royalty, musicians, artists, poets, and every kind of people enjoyed them.

In his opera productions Lully spared no pains and no expense to make the finished work attractive. It was not enough for the music, the dancing, the playing and the singing to be of first quality. The costumes and sets also had to be perfect. Even the orchestra was sometimes dressed to match the period of the story. For some operas the costumes were so luxurious that the linings of the sleeves were made of cloth with gold threads. The scenery included palaces, temples, fountains, winding rivers, and even erupting volcanoes. Machines permitted magical things to happen: characters changed into streams, trees, or birds. Gods and goddesses appeared on chariots floating in the air or on a cloud.

All of this cost money, but no expense was too great for the King, who paid for all of the productions. He liked to impress other kings and foreign diplomats. Once some ambassadors from Russia were actually frightened by some of the magic that they saw on the stage and had to be reassured that it was not magic at all, but done by machines.

The success of Lully's operas made him even more a favorite with the King. Lully was a good businessman, and did not hesitate to take advantage of his opportunities. He was able to make a good deal of money, more than any other composer of opera, because the King finally issued a command that said no opera or ballet written by another composer could be performed in the opera house unless Lully granted his permission. If Lully did give his permission, he received a fee in return. When one of his own operas was performed, he was given all the money that was taken in at the box office.

Besides operas and ballets, Lully composed religious works and marches. His marches were so famous that when princes of other countries wanted a special march for their troops, they went to Lully for one. It was Lully who originated the three part form for the march that is used today. The first part is in march rhythm, the second is melodious, and the third is in march rhythm again.

The best known of Lully's religious works is "Misereri." In this Lully used solo singers, a double chorus and a full orchestra with trumpets and kettledrums. The king loved this work and when he found that his valet had never heard "Baptiste's great Misereri" he insisted that the valet see the very next performance.

So talented was Lully, and so adept was he at knowing what would please the King, that he never lost favor. Louis XIV was always faithful to him. One day an Italian ambassador brought a violinist to the King, someone whose playing astounded everyone. The King listened in silence then signaled to one of his own violinists.

"An air from *Cadmus,*" he ordered. When the music had finished, he said to the ambassador, "This is my kind of music, sir." *Cadmus,* of course, was one of Lully's operas.

The final bit of acclaim came when the King made Lully one of his secretaries. This was a high honor and generally only given to nobility.

Lully was a powerful and wealthy man. He loved luxury and lived in grand style. He had come a long way from the poor country boy who had played with the wandering musicians at a Florentine carnival. His mansion in Paris was decorated with works of art, paintings, gilt mirrors, crystal chandeliers and elaborate tapestries. He had several carriages and three horses. And he ate and drank well.

His death was caused by a strange accident. He always became excited when he conducted, and once as he was leading his "Te Deum," he accidently hit his toes with the cane he was using to beat time. His foot became infected and blood poisoning set in. He seemed about to recover when suddenly he took a turn for the worse and died.

Lully, the miller's son whose ambition had carried him to great power in the court of a great king, was given a magnificent funeral by that King. For a whole year after his death, the newspapers in Paris were full of poems in all languages honoring him. To his wife he left five houses in Paris, two country homes, sacks of diamonds, other jewels, and large sums of money.

To the world he left a priceless heritage of ballets, songs, twenty operas, the music to the comic ballets of Molière, religious music of great depth, and many stirring marches. His music is still played everywhere and much of it has been recorded by some of the most famous orchestras in the world.

François Couperin

1668-1733

IN SOME FAMILIES RED HAIR IS INHERITED. IN OTHERS
it is blue eyes. But in the Couperin family it was musical talent.

The first of the musical Couperins was Charles, a
merchant in Chaumes, a small town near Paris. In his
spare time, Charles was organist of the parish church
and took part in many of the musical activities of the
town. Because he loved music, he was delighted when
all three of his sons showed musical talent, and he saw
to it that they all received excellent training.

Louis, the oldest and the most talented, became the
organist of Saint-Gervais, one of the largest churches
in Paris, and also a violist in the court orchestra of
Louis XIV. François, the middle brother, also became
a good organist, but he is said to have liked his wine
too well, and he never achieved real success.

Charles, the youngest of the three, followed in his brother Louis' footsteps, and became both a violist and an organist. When Louis died at the early age of thirty-five, Charles was asked to fill both of his brother's positions.

Soon after Charles was settled in the organist's lodgings provided by the church council, he married Marie Guerin. Their only son, François, was born in 1668. By this time music was such a tradition in the Couperin family that Charles was determined that his son should be musical.

Fortunately he was not disappointed; François showed great talent at a very early age. Before he could even speak, he could pick out tunes on the harpsichord, and by the time he was six, he had learned to play so well that he was really a child prodigy. His father taught him the harpsichord, theory of music, and took him along each day to Saint-Gervais for an organ lesson.

Like his older brother, Louis, Charles Couperin died young. François was only eleven, and he and his mother were left with very little money. He was already an excellent organist, and on the basis of ability alone, the authorities of the church would have been willing to have him take over his father's duties, but he was much too young to assume so much responsibility. So, the organist Michel de la Lande was given Mr. Couperin's position until François reached the age of eighteen. In order to help the young boy and his mother, La Lande kept only three quarters of the money that was to be his salary and gave the rest to the Couperins. They were also given permission to remain in the organist's lodgings.

Young Couperin was fortunate in that an old friend

of his father, Jacques Thomelin, who was an excellent organist in a church near Saint-Gervais, took over his musical education. He saw to it that François heard many kinds of music and was given every opportunity to develop into a well-rounded musician. Once Thomelin arranged for him to be present at a performance of Lully's opera *Persée,* which was given to honor the birth of the Duke of Burgundy, the grandson of Louis XIV. Couperin never forgot the excitement he felt at being present on so important an occasion.

Couperin progressed so rapidly under Thomelin's guidance that when he was only seventeen he was permitted to take over the complete duties at Saint-Gervais, and was given the same salary that his father had received. However, it was not until he was twenty-one, four years later, that he was given the official title of "Chief Organist of Saint-Gervais" as well as the full possession of the organist's lodgings. He then felt completely independent and was able to marry his fiancée Marie-Anne Ansault.

Couperin had much to do in Saint-Gervais. He had to play for the morning and vesper services each day, as well as two performances on Sundays and special ones on holidays. But he also found time to compose, and in 1690, the year his first daughter, Marie Madeleine, was born, his first two organ compositions were written.

Couperin was anxious to have his first works published, but that was difficult in those days. First it seemed wise to have a recommendation from the former organist at Saint-Gervais; then he had to be sure that he would be able to raise enough funds to pay for the publication. Michel de la Lande, was enthusiastic about the works and wrote, "I certify to have examined the present organ pieces of François Couperin which I found very beautiful and worthy of being given to the public." But funds for publication promised to Couperin never materialized and he had to be satisfied with only a few manuscript copies of his compositions which were written out for him.

As a result of this unhappy experience, when he composed some trio sonatas two years later he did not present them as his own works. Instead, as he explained when they were finally published under his name with some other works in 1726, "The first sonata of this collection was the first I composed and indeed the first ever composed in France. It had a singular history. Delighted by the sonatas of Signor Corelli, whose works I shall enjoy as long as I live as also the works of Monsieur de Lully, I rushed composing one which was played in the place where I had heard those of Corelli. Knowing French harshness towards foreign innovations of any type and not too confident in myself, I did myself a good service by a slight prevarication. I pretended that a relative who exists in fact in the service of the King of Sardinia had sent me a sonata by a new Italian composer. The signature was my own with the letters mixed up so that it looked like *Pernucio.* The sonata was swallowed with enthusiasm. This encouraged me to write more, and my Italianized name brought me under my disguise a great deal of applause."

However, Couperin soon became famous enough in his own right that he no longer had to play games and mix up the letters of his name or worry about getting money to publish his compositions. In 1693 when his former teacher, Jacques Thomelin, died, his position as an organist in the King's Chapel was open. There was a contest, and Louis XIV, himself, listened to all the contestants and chose Couperin "as the most brilliant and the most experienced." After that Couperin was both organist of Saint-Gervais and one of the organists of the Royal Chapel.

Being an organist in the royal chapel gave prestige and importance to a musician in those days because the chapel was much more than just a place of worship; it was also a magnificent concert hall and many performances were given there. The organ was placed above the altar and on all sides were galleries for choir, conductor and orchestra. Couperin began to compose Masses and motets for performances in the Royal Chapel. These were heard by important people and his fame spread quickly.

In the chapel, another Couperin, François' cousin, Marguerite Louise, the daughter of his Uncle Louis, was a celebrated singer. She took part in several performances of François' religious works.

Couperin had other duties in the court in addition to being organist and composer of the King's Chapel; he was the court harpsichordist and master of the harpsichord for the royal children. One of his best pupils was the Duke of Burgundy, the grandson of Louis XIV; it was in honor of his birth that the opera Couperin saw as a boy had been given.

Couperin soon became as great a favorite of Louis XIV as Lully had been. But he was a quiet and simple man, not at all like the domineering Lully. Luckily, the King's tastes in people and in music had changed. Instead of asking for spectacular ballets and operas like those of Lully, the King now wanted quiet, soothing music for his private salon. Couperin wrote music for the harpsichord and chamber music for instruments

OBOE

such as the violins, viols, oboes and bassoons. Many of these compositions were performed at special Sunday night concerts that Couperin arranged.

Among the works played on these occasions were the *Concert Royaux,* dance suites in which special instruments were used to produce special moods. For example, the oboes and bassoons were suitable for merry movements, such as rigaudons and bourrées; the flutes were appropriate for tender and melancholy movements like the sarabandes; and the violins played all the passages that were lyrical and noble. Some of the suites were written for unaccompanied viols, and the soft soothing sounds of these instruments were exactly what the King now wanted.

When the King gave Couperin the title "Monsieur le Chevalier Couperin," which was equivalent to knighting him, Couperin was extremely pleased. The first opportunity he had to sign himself as "Monsieur le Chevalier Couperin" was on the baptismal records of his second daughter, Marguerite Antoinette, who was born in 1705. Soon after that Couperin was permitted to have an elaborate coat of arms. He proudly described it as having "the sun shining brightly from a blue sky studded with silver stars upon a golden lyre."

By 1710 Couperin was known as "François Couperin le Grand" as well as Monsieur le Chevalier Couperin. He was called "le Grand" so he would not be confused with his uncle François, and because he was already the greatest of the Couperins. Composers dedicated their works to him with words such as "Every year I come from the provinces to see and admire you and I never leave your presence without my mind being filled with a multitude of fine thoughts. The man is fortunate who has had the honor of being in your company."

Couperin was a busy man. Besides performing as organist in Saint-Gervais and in the Royal Chapel and as harpsichordist, teacher and composer for the Royal Court, he taught privately at his home. In time he became the most popular teacher in Paris, and many of his harpsichord pieces were written for his pupils.

Couperin wrote several kinds of harpsichord pieces. Some of them were groups of dances. Usually, composers grouped dances together in what they called "suites." But Couperin called his dance groups *ordres,* and instead of labeling them with the usual dance names—allemande, courante, sarabande, gigue and so on—he gave his such titles as "The Mysterious Barricades," "The Satyrs," "The Butterflies," "The Pastures," "Tic-Toc-Choc," and "The Windmill."

The explanation Couperin gave for the names was: "I have always had some object or person in mind when composing these pieces and have furnished the title suggesting what it was."

When one listens today to the slow chords of "The Majestic One," one can imagine the King walking slowly through his beautiful gardens in Versailles. In the piece called "The Dodo," which is similar to a nursery song, the rocking rhythms of the bass make it easy to picture a baby being rocked to sleep. Couperin wrote four books full of these lively *ordres*.

At the same time Couperin was composing his harpsichord dances, he was also writing a book that told how they should be played. In it, among other things, he gave definite rules for the playing of ornaments— little extra notes that the musician adds to the music as he plays—and he included a system of fingering. His fingerings included the use of the thumb, which no one had done before.

Johann Sebastian Bach must have used Couperin's music and book, for some of Couperin's ideas are included in *The Well-Tempered Clavichord*. Bach seems to have taught Couperin's harpsichord pieces to his pupils, because he copied the little piece "Les Bergeries" into the notebook of his wife Anna Magdelena, when he was teaching her to play. Bach and Couperin corresponded about musical matters, but their letters have been lost. Reputedly, the descendants of Couperin used these letters as lids for their jam-pots.

In *The Art of Playing the Harpsichord*, Couperin also gave homely hints to teachers and pupils. He suggested that six or seven was a good age for a child to begin the study of the harpsichord. He explained the correct position to assume at the keyboard, and he said, "It is better not to mark the beat with the head, body or feet, and as far as facial grimaces are concerned, one can correct oneself by putting a mirror upon the rack of the harpsichord."

Late in Couperin's life, there was a controversy over which was better, Italian music or French. Couperin tried to soothe over the argument by composing works that combined the Italian style of Corelli and the light melodious style of Lully. Couperin wrote two humorous compositions "The Apotheosis of Corelli" and "The Apotheosis of Lully," each as a kind of musical allegory. In "The Apotheosis of Corelli" Couperin wrote music very much in the style of Corelli. But in the "Apotheosis of Lully" he contrasted the two styles.

The story the music is supposed to portray begins with Apollo descending to offer Lully his violin and to take him to Parnassus; this music is in the style of Lully. When Lully arrives in Parnassus, he is entertained by Corelli and the Italian Muses, and here the style of the music changes to that of Corelli. Apollo finally persuades the two musicians that the union of French and Italian styles would make music perfect, and the two composers play duets.

When these two works were first performed at one of the Sunday night concerts, everyone was amused and interested. Couperin felt he had accomplished his purpose.

Although Couperin was happy in his work, he always looked forward to the musical evenings with his family in their home on "The Street of the Good Children." Both the Couperin daughters were excellent musicians, and there were always several cousins around to join in the music making. The younger of the Couperin girls, Marguerite Antoinette, had become such a fine harsichordist that when her father was not well, she substituted for him in the court.

Gradually Couperin's health began to fade, and in 1724 when he was 56, he resigned from his post at Saint-Gervais because he could no longer climb to his place at the organ. In order to keep the name of Couperin in Saint-Gervais he suggested that his cousin, Nicolas, the son of his Uncle François, be given the position.

Couperin died on September 12, 1733. He was buried in the Church of Saint Joseph in Paris, and on September 14 a service was held honoring "the renowned François Couperin le Grand."

Marguerite Antoinette was given her father's position as harpsichordist and teacher of the royal children. This was the first time in the history of France that a woman had held such a position. The musical direction of Saint-Gervais remained in the hands of the Couperin family for several more generations. After Nicolas died, his son Armand Louis and then his grandsons Pierre Louis and Gervais-François were all organists in Saint-Gervais. It was 1826 before the death of Gervais-François brought the Couperin musicians to an end.

Because of the beautiful music François Couperin le Grand left to the world, the name Couperin has not been forgotten. His four books of harpsichord pieces, his religious works and his chamber music are performed and recorded in Europe and in the United States regularly.

Jean-Philippe Rameau

1683-1764

THERE WERE ELEVEN CHILDREN IN THE RAMEAU family, the family of Jean Rameau, organist of two churches in Dijon, France. Of these, three had the musical talent of their father, one girl and two boys. In addition the boys seem to have acquired, along with their musical ability, a restlessness and a sense of adventure that had to be satisfied.

Claude, the younger of the two, was extremely adventuresome. When he was eighteen, he ran away from home and enlisted in the army. He was accused of looting and was sentenced to be hanged, but somehow the noose that was put around his neck had been damaged by rain and did not close as it was supposed to do. So he was left alive, but hanging from a tree.

A band of hussars passed by and noticed Claude's predicament. Amused and sorry for him, they cut him down and let him go free. With only a torn shirt to keep him warm, he went to a nearby inn, where the innkeeper also felt sorry for him and gave him clean clothes, food, and a cot to sleep on. But Claude had no place to go, and no money to get anywhere, until he made a few puppets out of his torn shirt, and held a public marionette show twice a day for a week. At the end of the week he had enough money to get home.

Back in Dijon he found that his father had died and his older brother Jean-Philippe was filling in at the organ positions. Claude, a fine organist, was given the positions permanently, and he soon married and settled down. His restlessness and his sense of adventure were satisfied, and he was ready for a routine life.

For Jean-Philippe Rameau, however, who had been glad enough when his brother returned to take over the organ posts, there was no such easy end to restlessness. He, too, had left home as a young boy. In fact, he was sent away at the age of seventeen because he had become infatuated with a young widow in the neighborhood. His father had not wanted him to marry her, so he suggested a trip to Italy.

Italy had not been what Jean-Philippe wanted, although it had given him a chance to study Italian opera. He had joined a group of traveling musicians as a violinist and with them had given concerts in Marseilles, Lyons, and other cities of southern France. In many of these cities Rameau had also played the organ.

In the next few years he held a number of positions, none of them for long. The first was as temporary music master at the Cathedral of Notre Dame in Avignon. Then a few months later he went to a better position as the organist in the Cathedral of Clermont. Here he was given a six-year contract, but he did not remain for the entire six years. Instead he went to Paris where he studied and also served as organist in several churches. Then when his father died in 1709, he had come home to hold the positions in Dijon.

From Dijon, after the fortunate return of Claude, Jean-Philippe went back to his earlier position at Clermont, where they seem to have been glad to have him back in spite of his earlier broken contract.

It was here, on his second stay in Clermont, that a further restlessness and a new kind of adventure opened to him. During his first stay, he had composed his first music, some pieces for the harpsichord and three cantatas. They showed unusual talent, and the cantatas were said to be the finest yet written in France. Now, on his second stay, the desire to compose and to really understand harmony and composition seized him.

With this new interest, Rameau embarked on a project that was to last the rest of his life. For his ideas in harmony were so new and his discoveries of such importance to him that they kept him constantly pressing on to achieve new things.

His work began after he had read a great deal about the science of sound and the theory of music. On this basis he wrote *Treatise on Harmony*. In his book he said, "It is harmony, not melody, that guides us. No combinations of melody can sound well without thinking of harmony."

This was revolutionary. Harmony is an arrangement of chords based on a single melody. At the time most music that was being written used what is called counterpoint. This is a combination of several melodies that balance or interact with each other to give interesting combinations of sound.

In his book Rameau went on to discuss the various kinds of chords and how they could be used. For example, he showed that a chord with the notes *CEGC* was the same chord as *EGCE* or *GCEG,* the sound was the same in harmony, although the pitch of the notes might be higher or lower, depending on what the lowest note of the chord was. The lowest version of a chord possible in a scale he called the root position. The chord that began on the second possible note (*EGCE*) was called the first inversion, and the one that began on the third note of the chord the second inversion.

Rameau identified three main kinds of chords that could be treated this way: the tonic, the sub-dominant, and the dominant. The root position of the tonic chord is always built on the first note of the scale; the root position of the sub-dominant chord is always built on the fourth note of the scale; and the root position of the dominant begins on the fifth note of the scale.

When Rameau had finished writing his *Treatise on Harmony,* he wanted to take it to Paris and have it published, but again he had a contract with the church in Clermont and the directors would not let him leave. Once more his old restlessness, his urge to be off and doing, would not let him stay in one place when there was something he wanted to do somewhere else. So the Sunday after his request to leave had been denied, he played so badly, with such dreadful discords, that a choir boy was sent up to the organ loft to tell him to stop playing. This was just what Rameau wanted; he left for Paris the next day.

Rameau arrived in Paris in 1722 and was fortunate enough to have his *Treatise on Harmony* published almost immediately. The book was read and the ideas were discussed, but his theories were not popular and he was not accepted as a composer. The people of Paris were not interested in new ideas in harmony. They were content to listen to the light, entertaining music of Lully. Before Rameau could be popular, he had to prove that he, too, could write entertaining music as well as a *Treatise on Harmony*.

Rameau was discouraged until he met an old friend, Piron, who was busy writing sketches to be performed at the Fair Theater in Paris. Piron asked Rameau to provide music for some of the sketches. One of these, "The Savages" became extremely popular, partly because of Rameau's music. He had used as his inspiration the rhythmic dancing of two American Indians, then appearing at another theater in Paris.

While Rameau continued to write successful music for the theater, he was busy with a second book of pieces for the harpsichord. He gave each of these a descriptive title such as "The Hen," "The Call of the Birds," or "The Tambourine." The music for each recalled the animal or object in the name. Some of them soon became very well known. "The Tambourine," especially, was very popular.

Rameau was now earning enough money to think of getting married. He had fallen in love with a young lady named Marie-Louise, who had a lovely voice and hoped to become a professional singer some day. She was only nineteen and he forty-two, but they had many interests in common, and when he asked her to marry him, she agreed. Her family approved of the match, and the marriage took place on February 25, 1726.

Soon after his marriage Rameau wrote a third book of pieces for the harpsichord. With this, his reputation as a composer grew even stronger, but before he could really be recognized as an important composer, he had to have an opera performed. Ever since the days of Lully, opera was the kind of music that the French people liked best. However, in order to have an opera produced in France, it was necessary to have a patron. Rameau was not a man to seek help; he was independent and did not like to be told what he could and could not do, as so often happened when a composer worked for a patron. But in 1731 he met one of the wealthiest men in France, La Pouplinière, and the two seemed to understand one another. This man was a great patron of the arts, especially of music, and he took pleasure in helping talented composers. La Pouplinière had several houses in Paris and additional houses in the country. At his castle in Passy, near Paris, he maintained an orchestra, and a staff of singers. Each week the singers gave a concert on Saturday, the orchestra played for Mass on Sunday morning, and the singers and the orchestra gave a large concert in the castle on Sunday evening. Rameau became the organist, conductor and composer for La Pouplinière, . and the Rameau family, which now included four children, lived wherever La Pouplinière lived.

In his new position, Rameau composed music for concerts, for the Church, for balls, ballets, banquets and receptions. And when necessary, he improvised on the harpsichord with such brilliance that distinguished guests listened in amazement.

But several years went by and there was no opera, the one thing Rameau wanted. Finally to celebrate his fiftieth birthday, his opera, *Hippolyte and Arcie* was given at La Pouplinière's castle in Passy for a special audience of distinguished guests. The opera was a success. When André Campra, a famous French composer of the time was asked how he liked it, he said, "There is enough in *Hippolyte and Arcie* for ten operas. This man will eclipse them all." However, when the opera was given its first public performance in Paris on October 1, 1733, it received a great deal of criticism. Many people still did not like Rameau's new harmonies, his difficult ornaments, and his unusual use of some of the instruments in the orchestra, especially the wind instruments. In the works of earlier composers, bassoons, flutes and oboes played the same parts as the stringed instruments, but Rameau gave each instrument a part of its own. Many listeners argued that Rameau's new ideas made his music too difficult to enjoy. As a result two camps were formed: on one side were the "Lullistes" who still preferred the melodious simple style of Lully, and on the other the "Ramistes," or followers of Rameau.

Rameau did not listen. He was more interested in discovering what he could do with his ideas than in what people thought of them. His next work, "Les Indes Galantes" was a geographical ballet in which there were elaborate scenes in Turkey, Peru, Persia, and in a North American forest. Although this work was full of bold harmonies and new rhythms, it was accepted more readily than the opera had been. Six months after the first performance of the ballet, every tune from the overture through the last gavotte had had words set to it and was known everywhere. Rameau also arranged some of the music from the ballet for the harpsichord and other instruments so that amateurs could enjoy playing it.

Next Rameau set to work on a very ambitious opera, *Castor and Pollux*. It was first performed on October 24, 1737. After the first performance, the opera had twenty-one performances on succeeding nights. This was unique in the history of Paris opera; finally Rameau's genius was being recognized.

The story of the opera was taken from Greek mythology; it tells the story of the twin brothers, Castor and Pollux. Castor had recently died and his brother was determined to rescue him from the underworld. But to do this he had to have the consent of his father, Jupiter. His father consented but on one condition—that Pollux take his brother's place. Pollux agreed and descended to the underworld prepared to do so. Castor, however, was unwilling to accept such a sacrifice. He returned to Earth for one day, and then joined his brother in the underworld. Jupiter was so moved by the display of brotherly affection that he restored them both to life and made them immortal. Rameau's music for the opera is elaborate, dignified, and beautiful. There are brilliant parts for the chorus, the soloists, the dancers, and for the orchestra.

Although *Castor and Pollux* was such a success when it was first performed, it was not given again in Paris until the beginning of the twentieth century. And not until January 12, 1965, did it receive its first performance in the United States. The audience and the critics in New York City, where it was done, were most enthusiastic. One critic said: *"Castor and Pollux* is indeed a masterpiece and a very remarkable work for its period. It has an orchestral score full of originality in which woodwinds, and especially the bassoons are prominent. Rameau was far ahead of his time in music. He was the first musician to clarify the theories of harmony."

After the first performances of *Castor and Pollux*, Rameau became really well-known. He was now able to write another book about harmony, and he opened a school of composition. Although many students wanted to study with him, he accepted only twelve. They met three times a week for a session of from three to five hours. The school gave Rameau an opportunity to pass on his ideas to pupils who would use them and in turn pass them on to others.

Rameau was now so well-known that he was asked to compose a work for the marriage of the Dauphin of France to the Princess of Navarre. He wrote an opera, *The Princess of Navarre,* which was given in great splendor at the Palace of Versailles. It was such a success that Rameau was made "Composer of the King's Chamber" and given a pension. After this, no event in the royal family passed without something of Rameau's being heard.

This led Rameau, always willing to experiment, down some new avenues of music. Although he was a serious man, he now learned how to make people laugh. His comedy-ballet *Platée* was based on the misadventures of the nymph, Platée, who had a following of frogs, cuckoos, birds, donkeys, and Jupiter, who had changed himself into an owl. Wobbling strings represent the croaking frogs, flutes imitate the cuckoos, and flageolets are the birds. The most amusing sounds of all were those made by the chorus of the frogs, birds, cuckoos, and donkeys when they became alarmed at the presence of the owl.

Then, just as Rameau was at the height of his success, a troupe of Italian singers, called "The Buffoons," came to Paris and presented a new opera by the Italian composer, Giovanni Battista Pergolesi. This was a tuneful, light work much in the style of Lully. Once again many people began to complain about Rameau; there were those who favored him and those who preferred the lighter music. The quarrel became known as "The War of the Buffoons." Even the court was divided. The King, Louis XV, was on the side of Rameau and the new French music, but the Queen sided with the "Buffoons" and Italian opera. The majority of the musicians in Paris were on Rameau's side, because they, too, felt it was time to try new things. However, Rameau's old friend and patron, La Pouplinière, sided with the "Buffoons" and a friendship of almost twenty-five years ended. The Rameau family moved back to their old house in "La Rue des Bons Enfants," "The Street of the Good Children."

Rameau, to whom the adventure of a new idea was still more important than the favor of people, now spent a great deal of time on his compositions and on several new books on the theory of music. He also accepted more pupils. His leisure time was spent in taking long walks in the beautiful parks of Paris. A tall, thin man, "more like a ghost than a man", as one observer said, he walked as if he were in a trance. He never noticed anyone; if a friend approached him, he seemed completely bewildered and did not know what to say. The longest sentence he is reputed to have spoken was directed toward the mistress of a barking dog. Rameau said, "Keep this animal quiet; he has such a disagreeable voice."

Rameau was never a friendly man. He was quick to quarrel, and he always told people exactly what he thought of them. Yet he was generally forgiven his bad manners because he was such a fine musician.

Just as he was about to receive another honor, "The Order of St. Michael," from the King, he became seriously ill with typhoid fever. On September 12, 1764, a few days before his eighty-first birthday, he died, and on September 13, he was buried in the Church of St. Eustache in Paris.

Even today Rameau's theories of harmony are important. The twentieth century composer, Paul Hindemith, wrote: "Rameau provided a theory of harmony and melody that was to be a guide for a long time to come." The music of Rameau is still studied and performed all over the world; his pieces for the harpsichord are now played on the piano as well as the harpsichord. His operas, especially *Castor and Pollux* are heard in Paris and in the United States, and only a few years ago the opera ballet *Les Indes Galantes* was restaged and was the rage of Paris.

Heinrich Schütz

1585-1672

IN THE 1590's ANYONE OF ANY IMPORTANCE WISHING
to spend the night in Weissenfels, Germany, stayed at
an inn called "The Bagpipe." And so it was to The
Bagpipe that the Landgrave of Kassel went one night
as darkness overtook him on his way home from a
journey.

While he was having his supper, he heard, coming
from somewhere in the inn, the sound of a young boy
singing. The voice was so beautiful and the song so
well rendered that the Landgrave could not help but
ask who the singer was. It turned out to be the young
son of the owner, a boy named Heinrich Schütz.

The Landgrave, who loved music, immediately offered to take the boy back to the school he had started
in Kassel for talented boys. Not only would the boy
receive excellent musical training there, the man ex-

plained, but he would also be taught languages, the classics, poetry, and mathematics.

The boy's parents did not know what to do. They had never thought of their boy as a musician, and did not much approve of the idea. But they did not wish to offend the Landgrave. So they told him they could not decide immediately. He advised them to think it over carefully.

Herr Schütz was quite wealthy. He had hired a tutor to teach his children; so it was not necessary for Heinrich to go away for a good education. On the other hand, it did not seem really wise to pass up the Landgrave's invitation. Such an influential man could provide a fine future for a likely young man. And Heinrich, himself, wanted to go. He loved music and the prospect of having some really good music teachers excited him. So in the end, the Schütz family decided to send their son to Kassel.

At the court school, the boys were kept busy. There were regular studies and choir practice every day. The choir of boys sang in the church four times a week. All the boys were also given lessons on various instruments.

But there was also time for fun. During special celebrations, like the baptism of a prince, they would parade down the streets of Kassel dressed in all kinds of fancy costumes.

Schütz liked everything about the school, but especially the music. He immersed himself in his studies until he was twenty-three. Then his parents, alarmed at the idea that he might become a musician, insisted that he join his younger brother George at the University of Marburg. He was to study law. Schütz did not want to become a lawyer, but he wanted to please his parents. So in April 1608, he entered the University of Marburg. It was not a happy time for him, for he did not like law. Music was his only interest.

When the Landgrave came to visit him, he complained bitterly about the time being wasted in senseless studies. He pleaded with the Landgrave to find a way for him to go back to music.

The Schütz family was determined that their son should not be a musician. But again, just as when Heinrich was a boy, the Landgrave won. He gave Schütz enough money to go to Venice to study with the Italian composer and teacher, Giovanni Gabrieli.

At first as Schütz studied with Gabrieli, he was discouraged. There seemed to be so much he did not know. He did not feel he was prepared to study with such a great master. But Gabrieli knew better. He saw that Schütz had a remarkable talent and convinced him that he could become a great musician. At the end of two years, Schütz was the best student Gabrieli had.

Even Schütz's parents seemed proud when he told them of his accomplishments, for they sent him enough money to remain for a third year. At the end of that year, he had published his first works, a group of madrigals. "The Italian Madrigals, Opus 1" showed the influence of Gabrieli and also of Gesualdo. Schütz used word painting as Gesualdo had. When the words were "he slumbers now," the music rocked back and forth to give the feeling of slumber.

It was just at this time that Gabrieli became very ill. On his death bed, as an indication of his special affection for Schütz, Gabrieli gave him his favorite ring. Schütz was so impressed and so touched he never parted with it.

Schütz now went back to Germany, confident that

he was about to become a musician. But his parents still had other ideas. They had decided that music was a good hobby, but not really a profession. So once again Schütz, although he was now a man of 28, was a dutiful son and went off to the University to study law.

The law looked no better now than it had before. It did not take much to lure him from his studies. When the Landgrave of Kassel, still interested in his friend, created a special position for him as second court organist, Schütz could not resist. He was there by Easter of 1613, less than a year after he had started law school. In order to earn more money, Schütz also became the Landgrave's private secretary and tutor to his children.

At the end of 1613 the Landgrave was invited to attend a music festival in Dresden. When he went, he took Schütz with him, and there Schütz conducted one of the choirs with such success that he was asked to come back in September and October of 1614. At the same time, the Elector of Saxony, who lived in Dresden and was very powerful in that whole area, was so impressed that he wanted Schütz to stay in Dresden. But Schütz was loyal to the Landgrave. He would not consider leaving his friend and benefactor's service without permission.

The Landgrave did not want Schütz to leave, especially when he was at last becoming important and bringing renown to Kassel. But the Landgrave did not feel he could risk offending the Elector. So Schütz remained in Dresden.

A year passed, and the Landgrave felt that he had been generous enough. It was time for Schütz to return to Kassel. The Elector of Saxony did not think the same. He was determined that Schütz should remain in Dresden. Seldom has there been such a quarrel between two rulers over one musician. In the end the Landgrave was afraid that the quarrel might lead to war, and this he did not want. So he permitted Schütz to remain permanently in Dresden. As a parting gift, the Landgrave gave Schütz a golden chain with a gold medal on it. Schütz evidently cherished this as much as he cherished the ring from Gabrieli, because he wears the chain in all three of his portraits which are still in existence.

With the battle over, in 1617 Schütz became Kapellmeister of the Dresden court, and there, except for a few journeys to other countries he remained for fiftyfive years. As Kapellmeister he had many duties: he was conductor of the orchestra, composer to the court, purchaser of instruments, and teacher of the choir boys.

Under Schütz, all music in Dresden prospered. The choir was better than it had ever been before. The quality of the music performed was higher. And musicians and music from other countries were imported to add variety and spice to the German music usually performed. The Elector was proud and pleased, particularly with the new music Schütz introduced which was written in the "Italian concerted style"; this meant that voices and instruments were used together.

In 1619 Schütz's first really important work, "Psalms of David" was performed. It was written in the Italian style Schütz had learned from Gabrieli, and was the first work of its kind composed by a German. One of the men who heard it then wrote: "This great music was performed by many musicians of the Elector of Saxony, our most precious lord; there were solo singers, choruses, two organists, four lutenists, gambas, trum-

TROMBONE

pets, trombones and two kettle drums. This was all presented under the leadership of Heinrich Schütz, the grandest, most forthright, most outstanding and most lovable person at the Elector's Court."

With his work such a success, Schütz felt that he could marry. So on July 1, 1619, he and Jungfer Wildechin, an eighteen-year-old girl, were married. A copy of Schütz's "Psalms of David" was sent along with each wedding invitation, an unusual gift from the groom to the prospective guest. Eventually two daughters were born, Anna Justina and Euphrosyne.

For the next few years things went well in Dresden. Schütz was happy, for all his life was music. He wrote compositions for baptisms, weddings, funerals, and gatherings of royalty in addition to his more serious works. He conducted religious music in the court church, which had been decorated in a lavish Baroque style. His secular music was played in an enormous room known as the Great Chamber; it was filled with valuable paintings, carvings, unusual instruments, and had several large and lovely crystal chandeliers, a ceiling covered with splendid paintings of the constellations, and plenty of room for an orchestra and a large audience. There were two organs in the room, one made of stone and other made entirely of glass. It was a magnificent setting. Everything was bright, and Schütz was happy.

But things were not to remain so. The Thirty Years War had begun in Germany in 1618. It did not actually reach Dresden until 1631, but changes began to appear as soon as 1623. Money was scarce. And for some reason the musicians were always the last to be paid. A few were dismissed because there was not enough money to pay them all. This caused Schütz great worry.

And in the midst of these worries, an even greater trouble came to Schütz. His wife died, leaving him alone with his two daughters. Schütz was plunged into grief. Fortunately, he did not have much time to dwell on his sorrow, for the eldest daughter of the Elector was to be married and music had to be composed and rehearsed for the occasion. The Elector particularly requested that there be an opera. There had never been an opera written in Germany, so the Elector felt it would be a fine way to impress his guests.

Schütz complied. The name of the opera was *Daphne,* and it was received with much enthusiasm. There is no way to judge its merits today because the only copy of the work was destroyed in a fire in 1760.

If the music was like some madrigals written at about the same time, however, called the "Opitz Madrigals," it must have been very lovely. The madrigals are still in existence and are very beautiful.

Schütz continued to work, and to worry about money and his musicians, but none of this helped him forget his wife. Everything in Dresden reminded him of her, and when the festivities of the wedding subsided and life returned to normal, he could hardly bear the emptiness. He wondered if a change of scene, a visit to another city perhaps, would help. Venice was a city of pleasant memories, so he asked the Elector for permission to go there for a while to study. Permission was granted, and Schütz left for Venice on August 11, 1628.

In Venice, Schütz lost himself in study. Italian music had been his early inspiration, and it still had the power to teach and to move him. Claudio Monteverdi was the most important musician in Venice, and it was to Monteverdi that Schütz went. He learned that Monteverdi was stressing solo singing in his music, although he still used a great deal of instrumental accompaniment. His *stilo concitato* emphasized excitement and dramatic expression in a way that Schütz found impressive. Monteverdi was also a great composer of operas, and for the first time Schütz had a good opportunity to listen to many operas and to learn new techniques for writing his own. Unfortunately the one he wrote in Venice has been lost, but his long religious work, *The Sacred Symphonies,* can still be heard. In the third part of this piece, the influence of Monteverdi's *stilo concitato* can clearly be heard.

It was a time of new learning and happy experimenting for Schütz. But it was also something more. It was a time of accepting and forgetting. Monteverdi, too, had lost his wife and had been left with two small children. It was good for each to learn that others shared their grief.

A poet of the time said:

Who is there now can tell here of our Schütz,
How deep in sorrow, how o'erwhelmed by woe?
How can he drive away his loneliness?

His healer was Italy,
The noble Monteverdi did show the path.

With many new musical ideas, and feeling a great deal happier about his own life, Schütz eventually left Venice and returned to Dresden. There he found that his girls had grown and were in good health, although both his father and his father-in-law had died and his mother was dying. Also, the destruction and discomfort of the Thirty Years War had come to Dresden. The court of the Elector of Saxony was no longer what it had been. There were few musicians, and those who remained were paid very little.

Schütz found one of his singers living in dreadful lodgings with scarcely enough to eat. He wrote to the Elector at once to plead for help for the man: "I learn that he lives like a sow in a pigsty, has no bedding, lies on straw, has pawned his jacket. His wife came to me yesterday and begged me for God's sake to render fatherly aid and help them get away. I find it neither praiseworthy nor Christian that in a land so highly esteemed, less than twenty musicians can or will not be supported . . ."

The letter was duly sent to the Elector, but there was no response. The Elector had other things to think about and other places to put his money.

When nothing was done, Schütz felt so sorry for the singer that he gave him money from his own pocket. He also helped other musicians. But Schütz was not wealthy himself. He had little to spare.

It was just at this time that Schütz received an invitation from the King of Denmark to go to Copenhagen to arrange the music for the wedding of Princess Magdalene of Dresden to Crown Prince Christian of Denmark. Schütz would accompany the Princess on the trip.

Schütz was happy to leave Dresden, but he was appalled that in spite of the hard times the Princess was being sent off with her mother, brothers, and a company of 532 persons in 274 carriages pulled by 479 horses. This, from a place that could not support twenty musicians decently.

At the wedding Schütz had full charge of all the musical activities. He composed music for plays, ballets, and a masked ball. Everything went well, and the King was pleased. He gave Schütz a portrait of himself, a golden chain, and a sum of money.

Schütz went home content that he had done his part well, but once again, bad news awaited him. His daughter Anna Justina, only seventeen years old, was dying.

With this new tragedy, a change came over Schütz. Though he eventually resigned himself to his sorrow, he became more serious. And because Dresden itself was no longer a happy city, there was no longer a place for the operas and gay music Schütz had once composed. Instead he turned to religious music, which seemed to solace his own grief and bring comfort to the people of an afflicted city. And it is for these works that he is best known today.

Among the works he composed at this time were the

"Small Holy Concertos." They were small because they required few musicians; he had only a few available to him. But his work continued to be beautiful and full of new inventions. In "The Seven Words on the Cross," for example, the part of the narrator was even put to music. Before this, narrative material had been chanted or recited. In the new work it was written like the recitative of an opera. The words from the Bible were set more freely to music than any other composer had dared to do before. And the work was scored for a variety of instrumental and vocal ensembles to give different effects where different meanings were intended.

Schütz continued to write primarily religious music and music for small groups, except for special occasions when other things were needed, until the end of the Thirty Years War in 1648. Then he once again began to compose secular music, although religious music continued to be the most important part of what he did. After 1648 he was able to use more musicians in all that he wrote than he had been during the war.

At the end of the war there was a new Elector of Saxony, Johann George II, a fine musician and a good friend of Schütz. He encouraged Schütz to continue his teaching and composing, even after he was an old man. When he was almost eighty, he composed "A Christmas Oratorio" to be performed for the Elector on Christmas Day, 1664. It was a young and sprightly work. Specific instruments accompanied specific singers, and instruments were symbols of the characters the singers were portraying. The angels were accompanied by gambas, the High Priest by trombones, King Herod by a trumpet and so on.

Schütz's last composition "Story of the Suffering and Death of our Lord and Saviour Jesus Christ" is his most famous. It is a setting for the story of the four Evangelists: Matthew, Mark, Luke, and John. It is in the simple old church style, instead of the more embroidered Italian style, for it uses only voices and no instruments at all.

By the time this work was completed, Schütz was half blind and hard of hearing. He could no longer go out and spent most of his time reading the Bible and other religious works. He died at the age of eighty-eight, very quietly, while his friends and pupils sang around his couch.

In the years that followed his death, the works of Schütz, especially his religious works, had a great effect on other composers. Because he did influence many other composers and was the first great German composer, he is now sometimes called the father of German music. But by 1736 he had been almost forgotten. It was not until 1834, when the German author Von Winterfeld wrote a book on Giovanni Gabrieli and spoke of the importance of Schütz, that there was a revival of interest. Musicians once more began to study his compositions. Schütz societies were formed in Germany and in other countries of Europe, and in the United States. In 1935, to celebrate the 350th anniversary of Schütz's birthday, his picture appeared on a German postage stamp. There are many performances and recordings of his major works, and even some of his lesser works, today all over the world.

Dietrich Buxtehude

1637-1707

THERE ARE FEW GREAT COMPOSERS WE KNOW SO
little about as Dietrich Buxtehude. Not one picture of
him seems to exist. And until recently it was even im-
possible to say with any certainty where he was born.
Three towns, in three different countries, claimed him:
Hälsingborg in Sweden, Helsingör in Denmark, and
Oldesloe in northern Germany. It has now been quite
definitely established, however, that he was born in
Hälsingborg in 1637.

Hälsingborg is a seaport town on the sound that
separates Zealand from Sweden. Although it is Swedish
today, when Buxtehude was born, it belonged to Denmark. Because of this, in musical circles, he is sometimes called "The Great Dane." He is considered to
be a German musician, however, because most of his
work was done in Germany.

The outline of his life is simple and not very complete. His father was the organist of the Marie-Kirche in Hälsingborg. But shortly after Dietrich was born, his mother seems to have died and his father became restless. He moved from one position to another until finally in 1641, when Dietrich was four years old, he became organist of the St. Olai Church in Helsingör, which is directly opposite Hälsingborg. There he remained for the next thirty-two years.

In Helsingör Herr Buxtehude married a lovely Danish woman, Hella Jasperdaater. As time went on, three other children were born into the family: Anna, Katherina and Peter.

Dietrich was the only one of the children who showed musical talent, as far as we know, and his father taught him organ as well as theory of music at an early age. Dietrich may also have attended the Latin School in Helsingör, where music was given special emphasis. After each meal at the school a chapter of the Bible was read and this was followed by choir practice. The choir sang at the church on Sundays and for special occasions. At Christmas time it was sent out caroling around the town.

Dietrich's father may have been his only organ teacher. But it is also possible that the boy may have studied with Johan Lorentz, who was a well-known organist in Copenhagen at the time. An old, but unconfirmed, story says that Johan Lorentz's father built the organ in St. Olai's Church and because of that Herr Lorentz and Herr Buxtehude were friends. One day Herr Buxtehude is supposed to have asked Herr Lorentz to listen to Dietrich play, and the visitor was so impressed he suggested that Dietrich go to Copenhagen to study with his own son Johan. Copenhagen was only twenty-five miles away, so the lessons were arranged.

In 1648, when Dietrich was eleven, the Thirty Years' War ended and composers and performers came from all over Europe to present their works at the Danish court. No doubt because of his father's position as an organist, Buxtehude had an opportunity to meet some of these men and listen to their works. Schütz and his followers were among those who came, and Buxtehude must have become acquainted with the new "Italian style" of composition that Schütz had brought back from his visits to Venice.

Aside from these stories and surmises, we know nothing more of his childhood and early training. The next definite information we have is that when he was twenty years old he was given the position of organist in Hälsingborg, the town of his birth. He did not stay there long, however, because he was so poorly paid. He could not support himself on what he earned. So in 1660 he returned to Helsingör where he was soon offered the position of organist at the Marie-Kirche. The salary there was more than twice the one he had received in Hälsingborg.

The years in Helsingör may well have been happy ones because the pastor of the church at the time, Justus Valentine Steman, was a great patron and lover of music. He undoubtedly encouraged Buxtehude in many ways. The young man remained at the Marie-Kirche for eight years and left only because on April 11, 1668, he was offered a much better job.

The new position was that of music director at the Marien-Kirche in Lübeck, Germany. It was an offer Buxtehude could not turn down. Lübeck was a beautiful city with tree-lined streets and richly decorated buildings and churches. The Marien-Kirche was the largest of all the churches in Lübeck, and its organ was reputed to be the finest in all Europe. Franz Tunder, Buxtehude's predecessor, had been a pupil of the great Frescobaldi. The retiring director's job had included not only being organist and composer for the church, but also being its general overseer, which meant that he was secretary and treasurer of the church, purchaser of all supplies, and general contractor for all church repairs. For this work he received the highest salary given to any organist in all Europe. Buxtehude gladly took over both the responsibilities and the salary.

He also took over something more. According to the custom of the times, he was expected to marry the eldest daughter of his predecessor. So on August 31, 1668, Dietrich Buxtehude, now thirty-one, married Margaretha Tunder, thirty-two. The marriage was a happy one, and eventually the Buxtehudes reared a family of five daughters and two sons, not one of whom became a musician.

Buxtehude remained at the Marien-Kirche for the rest of his life. Week in and week out, he performed at two services every Sunday, one in the morning and one in the late afternoon. And sometimes he played at other services during the week and at an early Sunday morning service. In addition in 1673, he started an extra series of performances called the *Abendmusiken* or "Evening Musicals." These were given the five Sundays preceding Christmas and followed the usual late vesper service on those days. Sometimes there was a cantata, with the choir singing, but often it was just Buxtehude playing some of his own works. At first these were given just for the people of Lübeck, but eventually there were visitors from all over Europe who came to hear him play and to hear his music performed. The people of Lübeck realized that it was to their advantage to have so many travelers coming into their city, so they offered to help Buxtehude with the expenses of the programs, which had been supported by offerings of the congregation. After that, the concerts became more elaborate. It was even possible to purchase new instruments. Buxtehude was especially

TRUMPET

proud of two trumpets "constructed in a singular manner such as had hitherto not been seen even in a prince's band." But the greatest attraction of all was still Buxtehude's own playing.

And so, in work and in family life and most of all in music, life must have passed quickly for Buxtehude until May 9, 1707, the day he died. He was buried on May 16 in the Marien-Kirche where he had spent forty years of his life, and was mourned for a time and then all but forgotten.

Fortunately for us, it is not really the events of his life that are important—the day to day happenings he knew, his appearance, or his small problems and triumphs. We do not know these things, but we have from him still the things that matter most: his ideas as they are embodied in the music he wrote. And these have never been altogether forgotten. For even in the days immediately following his death, for the several centuries that followed his death in fact, when he himself was seldom remembered, he lived on in the influence he had had on his pupils. Through them he was still heard and felt.

In 1703, for example, Johannes Matheson, a young organist from Hamburg, Germany, was invited to come to Lübeck to play for Buxtehude. He in turn invited his good friend George Frederick Handel, also from Hamburg, to join him. When these two young men, Matheson, 22 and Handel, 18, arrived in Lübeck, Buxtehude listened to them both. And undoubtedly, they heard him play and had much good advice from him. Although he seemed particularly impressed with Handel, the story has come down to us that either of the young men could have had the opportunity to become his successor. But whichever did, would have had to marry Buxtehude's oldest daughter, Anna Margaretha, as Buxtehude himself had had to marry the oldest daughter of his predecessor. Neither wanted the job if Anna Margaretha came with it; so both refused.

But both undoubtedly remembered Buxtehude and their time with him in the years to come.

Then several years later, at a concert given on December 2, 1705, in honor of the new Emperor, Joseph I, there was such a crowd that two corporals and eighteen privates were called to keep order. One man in that crowd was Johann Sebastian Bach, then a young man of twenty. He had walked 230 miles from his home in Arnstadt to hear the great Buxtehude play at this concert. Bach was so fascinated by what he saw and heard he wished only to become a pupil of the great master. Buxtehude listened to Bach and saw in him a budding genius; he was as eager to teach Bach as Bach was to be taught. So, although Bach had only a month's leave from his job in Arnstadt, he remained for four months, learning all he could. He almost lost his job, but the experience was worth it to him. Buxtehude also offered Bach the job in Lübeck. But just as Matheson and Handel had found Anna Margaretha a problem, so Bach, too, had no desire to marry her. He was in love with his cousin Barbara, and she was waiting for him in Arnstadt. Though he was flattered by the offer, he refused it.

Many other young men were attracted to Lübeck to study with Buxtehude. None of them became as famous as Bach and Handel, but a few of them were remarkably gifted. Nikolaus Bruhns, for example, was a talented young man who was already a fine violinist when he came to study organ and composition with Buxtehude. He was such a good student that some of his compositions were mistaken for those of his teacher. And once he gave a violin recital seated at the organ, accompanying himself on the pedals of the organ. No doubt this, too, showed the influence of Buxtehude, for he was known to do amazing things on the organ pedals.

The young men who came to learn from Buxtehude undoubtedly learned much about organ technique from him. Some of them may have learned to play "pedal trills" and sometimes two trills at the same time— something no one had done before Buxtehude. And these techniques must have delighted people all over Europe who heard these pupils play. But the most important things his students took away with them and spread to all the varied places they went were probably his innovations in composition.

There were many composers before Buxtehude who had created chorales for use in the German Protestant Church. These were choral works based on religious folk melodies that had been handed down from generation to generation. But Buxtehude used these traditional tunes not only for the usual vocal works, but also as a basis for organ compositions. He wrote chorale variations, in which a familiar melody was presented in many different ways. He composed chorale fugues with the familiar melody as the subject that was repeated in each of the varied voices of the composition while the other voices played counterpoint to it. And most elaborate of all, he used chorales in what he called "chorale fantasies." Here he took just bits of the familiar tune and built and elaborated on them in a free and wholly original fashion, until sometimes it was difficult to even recognize the original melody.

Buxtehude also grouped preludes and fugues together. The preludes were pieces that showed off the ability of the performer. The fugues were often works of greater depth that expressed important musical ideas and rich melodies, although for some of these he used what he called a "laughing theme" which was based on one repeated note, *cccc* or *dddd*. The effect is a humorous one, and when played, it does sound like someone laughing. He also used dance forms in his compositions; one of his organ fugues is called "Jig Fugue." Bach seems to have been much inspired by all of these innovations for he wrote many combinations of preludes and fugues, and he even wrote a "Jig Fugue."

In addition to writing for the organ, Buxtehude composed beautiful cantatas. Many of these were written especially for the "Evening Musicals" in Lübeck. They were composed for solo voices or a small group of voices accompanied by various instruments. There might be, for example, three violins, two violas, three cornetts, three trumpets, bassoon, double bass and organ. Often each part of the cantata would have a different combination of instruments playing the accompaniment. Special effects were achieved with muted trumpets and muted violins. Echoes, a favorite device of the Baroque Period, were used in new ways. For example, in his cantata, "Rejoice Beloved Christians" the violins almost always echo the last three or four bars of each phrase of the voice part. This cantata and several others he wrote are widely performed today.

At other times Buxtehude composed music for the harpsichord; one such piece is a theme and thirty-one variations in C major known as "La Capriccioso." This composition was found in 1942 in Copenhagen in an album that had been handed down for centuries in the Danish family of Ryge. One member of the family, many years ago, is said to have been the choirmaster in the Cathedral in Copenhagen. Probably it was he who somehow acquired for the family the album called

Dietrich Buxtehude Klavier Vaerker. The theme for this set of variations is a folk melody called "Cabbage and Turnips." Although it is only in recent years that the piece has been found, it was not entirely lost. For Bach must have heard it, perhaps while he was a pupil of Buxtehude, and he perpetuated the idea in his *Goldberg Variations,* written in C Major, as was "La Capriccioso," both works have thirty-one variations; and the theme of the last of the *Goldberg Variations,* the "quodlibet," is "Cabbage and Turnips."

"La Capriccioso" is not the only lost work by Buxtehude that has recently come to light. He left many cantatas, organ works, a volume of harpsichord pieces, and chamber works that have been recovered only in the last few years. Most of them have turned up in old German libraries and are now being published. A society founded in Lübeck in 1932 is still busy preparing a complete edition of Buxtehude's compositions.

But for all the things that are now being uncovered, not one bit more information about Buxtehude himself has been forthcoming. Apparently even though the good citizens of Lübeck enjoyed his music, it never occurred to them that he and his music would be remembered and that future generations would be anxious to know more about him.

Even his family seems to have forgotten him. The man who finally married Anna Margaretha and became his son-in-law and successor never performed his father-in-law's works. The "Evening Musicals" were continued, but the works that had made them famous were no longer played.

It is only recently that scholars have come to recognize Buxtehude as the great organist, teacher, and composer that he was. One of these scholars has said,

"If Bach had never lived, would Buxtehude have been the greatest master of the organ?" The question will never be answered; for Bach did live and is undoubtedly the greater of the two. But there is no doubt that he was influenced by the man who was his teacher. Many of Buxtehude's toccatas, passacaglias, chaconnes, preludes and fugues are currently studied and performed by organists all over the world. In 1955 his chaconne in E Minor was used as a test piece in place of the customary Bach work for the examination of the American Guild of Organists. Side by side with this interest in his organ works is a renewed interest in his chamber music, harpsichord pieces, and cantatas. A great many of his works were recorded in 1957, to commemorate the 250th anniversary of his death. Perhaps at that time the lost organmaster really was found, for many of his organ pieces were again performed on the organ in the Marien-Kirche in Lübeck.

Georg Philipp Telemann

1681-1767

GEORG PHILIPP TELEMANN'S MOTHER WAS ALARMED about her son. Her husband was dead, and she alone was responsible for the boy, and he was being so difficult. The problem was that Georg Philipp had an unquenchable interest in music.

He had taught himself to play the violin, flute, and zither even before he could read notes. And before he started school in Magdeburg, the city in central Germany where he was born, he had entertained the neighbors with his gay tunes.

Once he did begin school, he studied reading, writing, Latin, Greek, and German poetry and did well in all of them. But his interest in music continued. It was true that he had taken a few organ lessons from a local teacher and had not enjoyed them, but this did not seem to hinder his continued interest in the subject as a whole. Georg Philipp said he did not enjoy the lessons because the teacher was old-fashioned, and the music running through his own head was much more joyful than the tunes the teacher expected him to play.

Now he was ten and his interest was greater than ever. His mother even suspected that he was doing some composing but could not really prove it. If he did, she did not know when he found the time for it, because she tried her best to keep him busy at other things all day long.

Georg Philipp's father and his grandfather had both been respected Lutheran ministers. It would be a disgrace, his mother thought, if her son were to become a worthless musician.

What Frau Telemann suspected was true. Georg Philipp was composing music. He was doing it at night in the attic after she was asleep. To be sure that he would not be found out, he signed his compositions with a false name.

The secret composing went on for a year or more. In that time young Telemann wrote several motets, some of which were sung by the boys in his school. He conducted the choir, and no one suspected that the music he was giving them was his own. The secret was kept until he wrote a short opera that was performed at the school, and word got out that he had written it.

His mother was beside herself. As Telemann, himself, wrote years later, "Oh, what a storm I drew upon my head with my opera. The enemies of music came in a host to see my mother and represented to her that I should become a charlatan, a tightrope walker, a trainer of monkeys. No sooner said than done, they took from me my notes, my instruments, and with them, half my life."

Georg Philipp was also sent away to a new school where he could concentrate on useful subjects like geometry.

The only problem with the new school was that the headmaster, Caspar Calvoer, knew as much about music as he did about geometry. He was quick to recognize Telemann's talent and encourage him to go on composing. He even taught his pupil many things about the theory of music. And on one occasion when a teacher who was to have composed a cantata for a popular festival became ill, Telemann, still only thirteen, composed it instead. He also conducted the piece. The performance was such a success that when the concert was over, men carried Telemann about on their shoulders.

After this performance Herr Calvoer encouraged his student more than ever. Each week Telemann had to compose a new motet for the school choir, as well as a composition for the church and one for the orchestra of the town.

When Telemann was seventeen, he was invited to study at the Hildesheim Gymnasium, a fine school near Hanover, which was then one of the largest music centers in Germany. There were several orchestras as well as an opera house in Hanover, and Herr Calvoer thought that it would be good for Telemann to be able to hear many concerts and many kinds of music.

At first Frau Telemann objected to the change because she was afraid her son would spend too much time on music, but finally Herr Calvoer convinced her that the Hildesheim Gymnasium was the best place for him to continue his education.

At his new school Telemann studied all the things his mother wanted him to study, but he also composed music for the choir and for the churches in Hildesheim. And he went often to Hanover to hear a concert or an opera. He was especially fascinated with opera because up until then he had heard little but church music. The head of the opera, a young Frenchman, took a fancy to Telemann and taught him many things about the opera.

Full of enthusiasm for his new found delight, Telemann set to work to write an opera of his own. But it was not to be. His mother heard of it and insisted that he return to Magdeburg immediately. She pointed out that he was now twenty years old and he must stop "wasting so much time on music" and prepare himself for a worthwhile profession. She wanted him to go to the University of Leipzig and become a lawyer.

Although Telemann was unhappy about his mother's decision, he was a dutiful son, and he agreed to carry out her wishes. In the fall of 1701, he left Magdeburg with a promise to his mother that he would have nothing more to do with music and would be a lawyer.

The promise was broken before he reached the University. On the way to Leipzig, he stopped in Halle, the home of George Frederick Handel. Telemann had been anxious to meet Handel for a long time. Although Handel was only sixteen, he was already a famous organist. The two boys became friends, and when they parted they promised to write to each other and exchange musical ideas.

Telemann went on his way, his mind full of music, but at the same time determined to try to forget it and pay attention to the law. When he arrived at the University of Leipzig and entered the room assigned to him, he noticed musical instruments hanging on the walls. His new roommate, he soon learned, was a great music lover and practiced the violin and the recorder whenever he had a free moment. Telemann said nothing about his own musical abilities and walked out of the room. As soon as he was out of sight, the roommate became curious about him. He lifted the top of Telemann's trunk, and the first thing he saw was a musical manuscript. He took it out, examined it, and much to his surprise saw that it was one of Telemann's own compositions.

When Telemann returned to the room, it did not take the roommate long to learn the truth. Telemann confessed that he was a composer but asked his roommate to please not say anything about it. The roommate did not carry out the request, however, for the very next day he showed the composition, a setting for a psalm, to the organist of St. Thomas' Church. The organist was so impressed that the choir of St. Thomas performed the psalm the following Sunday. The music was such a success that the Mayor of Leipzig called Telemann to his office on Monday. He gave Telemann money and engaged him to compose a new piece for St. Thomas twice a month. St. Thomas was then the most important church in Leipzig, so the assignment was really an honor for an unknown composer.

Telemann was delighted, but troubled. He had promised his mother that he would forget music. Yet how could he? When he left music behind, music came to him. He did the only thing he could: he wrote to his mother and told her what had happened. In the letter he said that he could not keep his promise because the only thing he wanted to do was to become a musician.

Perhaps the recognition Telemann had received from so important a person as the Mayor of Leipzig helped. Or perhaps his mother was tired of fighting what she could now see was a battle she would never win. At any rate Frau Telemann now gave her consent and her blessing and said that her son could be a musician.

Once Telemann was not burdened with other studies, he was able to work on his music much more diligently. He found that he could work quickly, perhaps because he had always had to work in spare moments and sometimes in secret. He composed music for St. Thomas, conducted the choir in the church, and became organist and choirmaster of still another church in Leipzig. He also composed operas for the city opera house. This caused a controversy because the older musicians in Leipzig thought that a church composer should not write operas. But Telemann won; he continued to write operas, which were performed, and he did not give up his church work.

But even this was not enough. Now that music had become his life, he could not seem to do too many things. There was always time for one more. He organized a student orchestra, "The Collegium Musicum," which gave weekly concerts. The orchestra's performances became so popular that people came from other cities to hear it play.

After Telemann had been in Leipzig for three years, he was invited to be kapellmeister to the wealthy Prince Erdman von Promnitz in Sorau, a town in the Prussian province of Brandenburg. Telemann accepted the offer and in 1704 he went to Sorau. The Prince, who was a great music lover, had recently returned from France, bringing back with him French ideas and French music. He tried to imitate all the splendor of the court of Louis XIV, and his court became known as "Little Versailles." Telemann loved the French atmosphere and above all he loved the French music. He studied the French works diligently, and in two years he composed over 200 overtures in the style of Lully.

Together with French music, Telemann also studied Polish music. The Prince spent several months a year in Cracow, Poland, and he always took Telemann along. In Cracow, Telemann became fascinated with the rhythms and the instruments used in Polish music. In a letter to a friend he wrote, "I have heard as many as 36 bagpipes and 8 violins playing together. One can hardly believe what wonderful ideas these bagpipers and fiddlers improvise while the dancers rest. In a week an observant person can pick up enough ideas to last a lifetime." Telemann did not spend a lifetime using what he had heard, but he did write some music using the lively Polish rhythms. Among these compositions is a collection of dances to be played on the recorder.

Although Telemann enjoyed the gaiety of his life with the prince in Sorau and Cracow, he stayed only four years, and in 1708 accepted a position in the court of the Duke Johann Wilhelm in Eisenach. There Telemann was kapellmeister to the court, first violinist in a new orchestra of the city, and secretary to the Duke. All of these positions together gave him a fine income, which he needed because he had been in love for some time and wanted to marry. His fiancée was Louisa Julianne Eberlin. Her father was a musician at the court in Sorau; he liked Telemann and was happy to give his consent to the marriage. So at the end of 1709 Luisa and Georg Philipp were married.

The young couple made their home in Eisenach. Telemann was happier than he had ever been. His wife made his home pleasant, he liked and enjoyed all his jobs, and he had good friends in Eisenach. His best friend was Johann Sebastian Bach, who had asked Telemann to be godfather to his second son, Philip Emanuel.

Unfortunately Telemann's happiness did not last. On January 2, 1711, only nine weeks after Luisa had given birth to their first child, she suddenly became very ill and died. Telemann was overwhelmed with grief. His only comfort was his work. He threw himself into his music. He played the violin and also other instruments at court, he directed a new orchestra and chorus in Eisenach, and he composed a great deal of music. It was at this time that he composed some of his "Tafelmusic," table music, designed to be played or sung for private or official dinners. Other music

RECORDER

written at this time includes: chamber music for re-corders, flutes, oboes, trumpets, strings and harpsi-chords; serenades for weddings of the nobility; and "Captain's Music" to be played and sung at the side of the piers when distinguished captains arrived home from journeys.

In spite of all of this work, Telemann was unhappy. He missed Luisa and longed for a change of scene. So when he was offered a position in St. Paul's Church in Frankfurt, Germany, in 1712, he and his small daughter left Eisenach for that city.

About a year and a half later, he decided to marry again. He was lonely and he found it difficult to bring up his daughter all by himself. His new wife, Maria Katherina Texton, came from a prominent family in Frankfurt. As the years went by she had seven sons. It was fortunate that Telemann could work quickly and accomplish a great deal in a short time. The family needed all the money he could earn.

In Frankfurt, Telemann composed all the music for the performances at St. Paul's Church, and at the same time still composed music for churches in Eisenach; he organized an orchestra, which gave two concerts a week; and he taught some of the best students in the city.

Telemann taught his pupils new ideas. At a time when counterpoint, the use of two or more melodies at the same time, was the important thing in German music, he taught that an appealing simple melody was more effective than several melodies going on at the same time. He would say, "Don't listen to the old fellows who say that counterpoint is the most impor-tant part of music." He wrote the kind of music that was easy to understand, and his pupils did the same.

Telemann's music slowly became known all over Europe. Many foreign musicians visited him, and new positions were constantly being offered to him. But he was treated well in Frankfurt, his wife encouraged him to remain there for it was her home, and so that is where he stayed for a long time. Eventually, however, when a far better position was offered to him in Hamburg, Germany, he did decide to move. In October, 1721, the Telemann family went to Hamburg.

In Hamburg, Telemann again had many responsibilities. He was director of music at the Johannes School, he gave lectures on music history at the Hamburg Singing School, he was director of the opera house in Hamburg, and he composed music for five churches. Sometimes he wrote five different religious cantatas in one week. And besides writing cantatas for the church, he composed secular cantatas for the boys to perform at the Johannes School. One of these, still performed today, is "The Schoolmaster." In this cantata, which might even be called a children's opera, Telemann describes a teacher trying to teach a mischievous group of boys to sing a cantata. They are so busy talking that half the time they either forget to come in or they come in at the wrong time. Telemann also pokes fun at the teacher who isn't familiar with the cantata he is teaching and blames his mistakes on his pupils. "The Schoolmaster" ends with the teacher and the pupils imitating the sounds of jackasses, "Eeeh, aah, eeh," and singing in a monotone, "All the jackasses who have no feeling for the beauty of music . . ." This cantata as well as others that Telemann composed at this time became popular immediately. Many were easy enough to be performed at home for the entertainment of a family.

No matter how much work Telemann had to do, he was always ready to accept more. In 1722 he was invited to become Chief Cantor at the St. Thomas Church in Leipzig. This was a job he had wanted for over twenty years. He felt especially honored because out of the six important German musicians who had been interested in the position, he was the person chosen for it. He went to Leipzig, but after six months he became lonely for Hamburg and went back.

The people in Hamburg were so pleased that he had chosen their city over Leipzig that the city council voted to make Telemann's orchestra larger, to make his salary higher, and to perform more of his compositions.

Now in addition to all of his other work, Telemann founded the first German music journal. The magazine *The Faithful Music Master* was published in twenty-five installments, and each one was a music lesson illustrated with the best music being composed in Germany at that time.

With the constant increase in his work, Telemann's health became bad. He had frequent asthma attacks and his eyes troubled him. To make matters worse, his wife left him, never to return. Fortunately, just at this time he received an invitation to come to Paris.

For many years Telemann had wanted to hear French music performed in its native country. Now his opportunity had come. It was a pleasant journey. Not only did he hear French music, but he heard French musicians playing his own works. Some of his compositions were even published in Paris. Never before had a German composer been so honored.

Telemann spent eight months in Paris, and when he returned to Hamburg, he was treated like a celebrity.

He was named a member of the "German Society," the most prominent cultural organization of the time, and his compositions were performed on every occasion. Though Telemann was now an old man, and his eyes were nearly blind, he could not stop working. On the score of a psalm, he wrote when he was eighty-one, he said, "With an ink too thick, with a foul pen, with bad sight in gloomy weather under a dim lamp, I have composed these pages. Do not scold me for it." Even in his later years Telemann preserved the youthful spirit of his music. His friends said that "his work advanced with youth not age."

In his old age Telemann had two loves: music and flowers. He took care of his flower garden by himself, and he was always happy when Handel sent him rare plants from England. Telemann and Handel had always remained the best of friends.

On June 25, 1764, at the age of 86, in the midst of working on a new composition he fell ill and died within a few hours. It was almost as if he could never make up for the years in his childhood when he had to write in secret and could never get down all the joyous tunes that ran in his head.

Telemann had become such an important person in Hamburg that a proclamation was issued by the city council announcing his death. All Hamburg mourned for him.

Telemann's new way of composing music with a light and appealing melody done in a bright and easy style made him the most popular composer in Germany during his lifetime.

However, for many, many years after his death his music was completely forgotten. Only in the twentieth century has the music of Telemann once more become important.

Yet Telemann was definitely an innovator in music. He was the first composer to use a clarinet in one of his works. He wrote comic opera in Germany for the first time; and some of his ideas foreshadowed the work of Haydn and Mozart. The first compositions Mozart's father taught him are reputed to have been minuets of Telemann.

Among Telemann's works that are now performed and recorded are: sonatas for recorder, flute, oboe, strings and harpsichord; suites describing stories, for example, "Don Quichotte"; twelve sets of religious cantatas; secular cantatas like "The Schoolmaster"; operas; and overtures.

Henry Purcell

1659-1695

MUSIC HAD ALWAYS BEEN IMPORTANT IN ENGLAND. It was heard on every street corner and in every home and castle. Anyone who could afford to own an instrument did, and a common entertainment in the home, either for the family alone or for the family and guests, was a small concert in which everyone present took part. This was true from the time of the Middle Ages until after the reign of Queen Elizabeth I.

But times changed. Charles I, who came to the throne not long after the death of Elizabeth was not a popular king, and he was beheaded. He was replaced by Oliver Cromwell, who assumed the title of Lord Protector, not King. Cromwell represented the Puritans, a group that wanted to reform the church and the country. They felt that there had been too much merriment, too much gaity, and too little attention paid to serious things. They did not trust music, for too much of it was gay and did little to encourage serious thinking. They did not even approve of church music. They preferred long sermons in church.

And so for ten years, from 1650 to 1660, musicians were driven from the country, musical instruments destroyed, and much music itself burned and lost.

Then in 1660, there was again a sudden change. Charles II came to the English throne, and with him music came back to the country. Charles II had been abroad in France, where he had heard the music of the young Lully and the twenty-four violins of the court of Louis XIV, the Sun King. One of the first things Charles II did was to organize a band of twenty-four violins for himself. At the same time he saw to it that older organizations for lutes, viols, and voices, including the choir of the Chapel Royal, were restored. And for all of these, music in the French style, which Charles II had come to enjoy, was the accepted thing.

Among the members of the choir of the Chapel Royal were two brothers, Thomas and Henry Purcell. They came of a family with a long musical history. For one hundred and fifty years the Purcells had been musicians, and Thomas and Henry were both talented and accomplished.

The younger of the two, Thomas, had a son, Henry, born in 1659, the year before the return of Charles II. It was expected that young Henry would be a musician, and he did not disappoint his family. He showed a great deal of talent as a very young boy. And fortunately, he was born at a time when there was no reason why he should not have good training. In fact, because for ten years music had been neglected, there was a great demand for young boys who had musical talent.

Many musicians had fled the country and none had been trained in the musicless years, so there were not nearly enough musicians to satisfy the needs of the king and the people, once music was allowed again.

Young Henry was taught to play the recorder, lute, and harpsichord, as well as a little about the theory of music before he was even five years old. By the time he was six, he had already composed a three part song, "Sweet tyraness I now resign."

When Thomas Purcell showed Henry's composition to Captain Cooke, who was the "Master of the children of the choir of the Royal Chapel," Cooke was so amazed that he wanted Henry to join his choir at once. In those days women were not allowed to sing in the church choir, and the high parts in the music had to be taken by boys whose voices had not yet changed. These boys, generally twelve in number for the choir of the Royal Chapel, were housed in a special school.

Mr. Purcell was quick to see the advantage of such a school for his talented son, so he consented to his becoming a member of the group. Henry was soon fitted out with the school uniform, special costumes that designated the boys as "servants of His Majesty." The Lord Chamberlain's records for that time give the following description of the costume: "For each of them one cloak of scarlet cloth lined with velvet, one suit and coat of the same cloth made up and trimmed with silver and silk lace, after the manner of our footmen's liveries, and also to the said suit three shirts, three half shirts, three pairs of shoes, three pairs of high stockings, two hats with bands, three handkerchiefs, three pairs of gloves, and two pieces and a half of ribbon for trimming garters and shoe strings." It was evidently important that the boys dress well.

The boys were well taken care of in other ways as well. They were taught not only to sing but were also given instruction in the lute, recorder, viols, organ, composition of anthems, and regular school subjects such as Latin and literature. Captain Cooke supervised all of this and saw to it that the boys obeyed all the rules of the establishment, including the one that sent even the oldest of them to bed at eight o'clock at night.

Although Henry was for a long time the youngest member of the choir, he made more progress than any of the boys at the school, except possibly the much older John Blow and Pelham Humfrey, who also became famous musicians. Henry seemed to do everything well. When he was eleven, he was the one chosen to compose a special anthem for the King's birthday. It was called "Address of the children of the Chapel Royal to the King and their Master Captain Cooke on His Majesty's Birthday." This was later published in a book called *Choice Ayres, Songs and Dialogues.* Like many other songs and anthems Purcell wrote during his student days, it is still sung today.

Charles II took a very personal interest in the boys in the choir school and tried to see that they received the best musical education possible. Consequently Pelham Humfrey was sent from the school to Paris to study with Lully. He was seventeen when he went and nineteen or twenty when he returned full of ideas about music in the French style. Shortly after he came back Captain Cooke died and Humfrey became his successor. He immediately began to include a great deal of French and Italian works in the concerts the choir gave, and he also taught the boys to compose in new styles.

Unfortunately only two years after he became master, Humfrey died. John Blow, another talented pupil at the school, took over. Just at that time Purcell's voice was changing. He could not continue singing with the choir, but his talent was so great he was permitted to stay at the school and learn from Master Blow. The two became great friends, and in later years John Blow was always proud of the fact that he had been master of the famous Mr. H. Purcell.

In those times, although schooling and training were important, working was important, too. Not many boys continued their education into their late teens or early twenties without also doing some kind of work. Purcell was a little past fourteen when he was given his first position. He became the assistant to Mr. Hingston,

FLUTE

"the keeper, maker, mender, repayrer and tuner of the regalls, organs, virginals, flutes and recorders." Purcell received no money for work. It was a kind of apprenticeship for him, and it did teach him a great deal that was useful in later years.

Purcell must have learned his job quickly, for the next year, when he was only fifteen, he was put in charge of keeping the organ in Westminster Abbey in tune. For this he was paid two pounds for a whole year's work. The pay was small, but Purcell was proud of what he had been given to do. It was a great honor for a fifteen-year-old boy to tune the most important organ in England.

Two years later, when Purcell was eighteen, Matthew Locke, who had been composer for the King's violins, died. A contest was held to choose his successor, and Purcell was chosen. He was so young that many people did not believe that he had won the competition fairly. He had long been a favorite of the King, and besides his family was friendly with the Locke family. This, rather than his talent, seemed to explain the choice. But soon Purcell proved that he was indeed the best of those that had competed.

Purcell took up his new duties with enthusiasm. They gave him a chance to try doing a great many different things. And in the next few years he seemed determined to make up alone for all the years there had been no music. He wrote airs and dances for singing and dancing at court. Many of these were later published in the book *New Ayres and Dialogues*. Because the King loved to sing duets, Purcell wrote many especially for him. The King's partner in the duets was the Reverend John Gostling, who sang with Purcell's father in the Chapel Royal. Gostling could sing, it was said, lower than any other bass in all of England. And if the pieces that Purcell wrote for him are any indication, this was probably true. The Duke of York accompanied the King and Gostling on the guitar.

Purcell also wrote pieces that, for want of a better name perhaps, were called odes. They were pieces written for special occasions or to commemorate special events. There were birthday odes, wedding odes, odes to welcome the King home from trips, and sometimes even odes for matters of public importance. On one occasion a plot known as the "Rye House Plot" was uncovered. A group of men had planned to overthrow Charles II. The men responsible were executed, and Purcell wrote an ode about the plot called "Fly, Bold Rebellion."

During this time, the anthem was the most important kind of English church music. And these, too, Purcell wrote. His were different from any that had been written before. They had catchy rhythms and pleasing tuneful solos for the singers. Instead of just using the organ for accompaniment, Purcell added a stringed orchestra. Some people objected to these new ideas and felt that his music belonged not to the church, but to the tavern or theater. But most people enjoyed it. It became fashionable for people to go to church just to hear one of Purcell's new pieces.

Not all of Purcell's anthems were meant for the church. On one occasion he wrote one to express gratitude for the safe return of the King from unexpected danger. The King and some of his friends had taken the King's barge for a pleasure trip to the Kentish Coast when they ran into a terrible storm and were almost shipwrecked. The King and his companions got down on their knees to pray that they might be saved, and by some miracle they were. When they returned home safely, Purcell composed the anthem "They that go down to the Sea in Ships." In it he wrote a special part for John Gostling reaching down to low *d;* this was to show how low in spirit the King and his party had been when the ship was in such danger. The King was deeply moved by Purcell's anthem, and became even more fond of him.

It was at about that same time that John Blow, Purcell's old teacher, resigned as organist at Westminster Abbey so that Purcell might have the job. Blow felt that Purcell was more capable than he. Purcell felt honored and humbled by the generosity of his teacher.

With so many jobs, Purcell could well afford to get married. And the next year he did. His bride's name was Frances Peters. The young couple moved into a house in Great Anne's Lane in Westminster, London.

That same year, always anxious to try something new, Purcell wrote music for a play. As it turned out, this was a highly successful venture. His music became very popular, and in the next fifteen years he was asked to write music to accompany over forty other plays.

Purcell seemed to have unlimited energy, and time must have stood still for him, for in 1691, in addition to being court composer, composer for the theater, and organist at Westminster Abbey, he was also chosen to be one of the three organists at the Chapel Royal. It was here he had worked and studied as a boy, so the new job brought back pleasant memories.

In composition he continued to pour out great numbers of works and in great variety. In 1682 he wrote a group of fifteen fantasias for the viol. A *fantasia* is a piece in which a composer let his fancy rove as it will. The music generally does not have a set structure. However, in the fantasias of the sixteenth and seventeenth centuries composers did follow set rules of counterpoint. Purcell's fantasias are unusually beautiful and show him to be a master of counterpoint.

For relaxation Purcell sometimes joined friends for an evening of singing and merriment at a tavern. There the men sang catches—rounds written for three or more unaccompanied voices. For such occasions Purcell wrote many jolly songs. Sometimes the words were so funny the men had to stop singing because they were laughing so much. Fifty of these catches were later published in a book entitled *Catch that Catch Can, The Pleasant Musical Companion.*

While Purcell was writing catches purely for fun, all kinds of music for the King, for the church, and for the stage, he was also composing serious works for himself. The sonatas he composed in 1683 set precedents for future composers. Purcell's sonatas are for the violin instead of the treble viol as was customary; this was the first time serious music had been written for the violin in England. Written in the Italian style, and not in the French style which other English composers were using, the sonatas used Italian musical terms such as *adagio, presto,* and *largo.* Never before had this been done on an English score. In his preface to the sonatas Purcell wrote: "I shall say but a few things by way of preface concerning the following book and its author, for its author has faithfully endeavored a just imitation of the most famed Italian masters principally to bring that sort of music into vogue among our countrymen."

In February 1685, King Charles II died, and the

Duke of York was crowned James II. For the coronation Purcell composed two anthems, and both he and his teacher John Blow joined in the singing of them. They were performed by a great consort of voices and instruments.

Soon after the coronation James II added to Purcell's already full schedule by making him "the harpsichord player for the King." In honor of his new job Purcell composed "A Choice Collection of Lessons for the Harpsichord." Among the pieces in this collection are eight suites that Johann Sebastian Bach must have studied, for six of the suites he wrote for the clavichord were much influenced by them. These suites are even called "The English Suites."

James II was an unpopular king, and he was finally forced to flee the country by the people and the Parliament. In April of 1689 William III and Mary II were crowned, and again there was an elaborate coronation ceremony. This time Purcell was in his usual place in the organ loft. It was the custom that people who wanted to watch the ceremony could pay to watch from the organ loft. The organist collected the money, but he had to turn it over to the treasurer of the Abbey. For some reason Purcell collected the money but did not turn it over. Only when he was threatened with loss of his job and a suit to collect the money did he pass on what he had collected. Perhaps with all the chores he had to do and all the things he had on his mind, he just forgot.

At any rate, the episode did not seem to damage his reputation. He soon became a great favorite of Queen Mary. He was often asked to play for her, either alone or with a group of court musicians. The songs played on those occasions were always his. On one occasion, however, she asked for a Scottish ballad called "Cold and Raw." Purcell had never heard of it, but one of the ladies of the court had, and she sang it, accompanying herself on the lute. When Purcell saw how much the Queen enjoyed the melody, he incorporated it into the birthday ode he wrote for her next birthday.

As the years went by, Purcell became more and more famous. Everyone knew his music. And well they might, for he had written so much and so many kinds, that no one could escape. But most popular were his songs and his music for the theater.

It seemed natural then for Josiah Priest, dancing master and head of a girls' school, to ask Purcell to compose something for the girls to perform at the end of the school year. Priest wanted something that would not be too long and difficult, and something the girls would enjoy doing. In response Purcell composed his first opera, the first opera to be written in England. It was short, only an hour in length, and was based on the tale of Dido and Aeneas from the works of the Roman poet Virgil. Purcell's friend the poet Nahum Tate wrote the libretto.

The story was a romantic one, one that was sure to appeal to young girls. Aeneas, the hero, was fleeing from ruined Troy to Italy. In a storm his boat went off course and landed in Carthage, North Africa. Carthage was ruled by the beautiful Queen Dido, who fell madly in love with Aeneas. He too fell in love, and all was going well until a band of witches appeared and ordered Aeneas to leave the country. Aeneas said good-by and Dido, in a frenzy of grief, killed herself.

There are many charming songs in the opera. The witches sing "Harm's our delight and mischief our skill," a chorus that has always pleased the audience of opera. Most famous of the songs, however, is "When I am laid to earth" better known as "Dido's Lament." It is one of the finest arias in all opera. Especially interesting is the bass accompaniment. At that time Baroque composers, and especially English Baroque composers, used what is known as a ground bass. This is a tune of four or eight measures that is repeated over and over again. The ground bass in "Dido's Lament" is especially lovely, and together with the unusual melody, the song creates some striking harmonies.

From that time on Purcell wrote more and more music for the theater. *Dioclesian, King Arthur, The Tempest,* and *Fairy Queen* are only a few of the titles for which he wrote the music for the stage presentations.

Fairy Queen was his longest work of this kind. The story of the work was based on Shakespeare's *A Midsummer Night's Dream.* There were over fifty musical numbers in the work, and the entire play took over five hours. In the course of the presentation swans changed into fairies, a bridge dissolved, peacocks and strange birds passed over the stage, Phoebus galloped through the clouds in a chariot drawn by four white horses, waterfalls were created, and fountains, fireworks, monkeys, exotic wildlife, and Chinese dancers all cavorted in time with Purcell's music.

Unfortunately after the second performance, the music was lost. It was sought everywhere but did not reappear until over two hundred years later.

At the same time Purcell continued to compose for the court. He wrote jigs and bourrées and minuets and hornpipes. Each spring he composed a birthday ode for the Queen. It was a very busy life.

In December of 1694, during a severe epidemic of smallpox, the Queen became very ill and died. She was well liked and was greatly mourned. For her funeral Purcell composed the anthem "Thou Knowest Lord the Secrets of Our Hearts."

In order to forget his grief, because the Queen had been a real friend to him, Purcell began to work on an elaborate hymn of praise "Te Deum and Jubilate." It was written for double chorus and orchestra. When it was finished, it was and still is the grandest hymn ever written in England.

All the time it was being written, Purcell was ill. He had been ill for some time, and he felt certain that he would not live. But he continued to compose. He wrote music for two plays, *Indian Queen* and *Don Quixote*. One of the songs for *Don Quixote* became very popular. Known as "Rosie Bowers," it was later printed in a collection of Purcell's works with the note that it was the last song he wrote.

As the year 1695 progressed Purcell became more and more ill. Finally on November 11, the eve of St. Cecilia's Day, one of his favorite celebrations since she is the patron saint of music, he died. He was buried on November 21 in the north aisle of Westminster Abbey, at the foot of the organ he had first tuned as a boy of fifteen. The same music that had been played at the funeral of Queen Mary was played at his funeral. In the London newspaper, *The Post Boy,* there was the comment "he is much lamented being a very great Master of Musick." Much more was said, but this seemed to sum up the feelings of all those in England who loved music.

Purcell was only thirty-six years old when he died. Yet he left more music than some composers who lived twice as long. And what is most remarkable, he left such an enormous variety of works. Most composers wrote several different kinds of music, but excelled in one. For example, Schütz excelled in religious music; Lully, in opera; and Corelli, in violin sonatas. But Purcell composed every sort of music, and all of it is good. He could write a popular tune as well as an anthem for a cathedral service.

It is his songs that are most remembered and most played today, however. He has sometimes been called "the father of English song." And no one who has ever heard "Dido's Lament" will wonder why. From the song he wrote as a boy of six, to the last song he wrote, his compositions were tuneful, beautiful, and attractive to the listener.

Glossary

Adagio—A slow leisurely tempo. Also music played at a slow tempo.

Air—A term for a song.

In French opera and ballet of the seventeenth and eighteenth centuries an air was an instrumental or vocal piece used to accompany dancing. In the eighteenth century composers often called the slow movement of a suite an "air."

Allemande—A stately court dance in Germany in the sixteenth century. There were four beats to the measure and the tempo was a moderate one.

In the seventeenth century the allemande was no longer danced but was used as the first movement of a suite.

Anthem—A composition for voices usually with a religious text and performed in church.

Purcell's anthems were not always for the church. For example, to celebrate the safe return of the King and his party after a near shipwreck he wrote the anthem "They that go down to the Sea in Ships."

Aria—A song or melody sung by one person with an accompaniment. It gives the singer a chance to "show off" his voice. Arias are found in operas, cantatas and oratorios.

Ayre—A late sixteenth century type of English song. This was usually accompanied by lute, theorbo or bass viol.

Basso Continuo—A continuous bass written in a system of musical shorthand. The composer put down the notes with numbers above or below them. These numbers indcated the chords that were to be played. For example, if the numbers were $\frac{5}{3}$ the upper note of the chord was a fifth, or five notes up from the bass note, and the lower note was a third, or three notes up.

Bourrée—A rapid dance of French origin with two beats to the measure. The tune always begins on the last beat of the measure. It first appeared in Lully's operas and ballets. However, in the late seventeenth and early eighteenth centuries the bourrée became a movement in a suite.

Cadenza—A brilliant section of a composition usually found at the close of a vocal solo or as a solo part of a concerto. It gives the performer a chance to "show off" his technique. Early examples of the modern cadenza found in the concertos of Corelli and Vivaldi.

Camerata—The name for a group of distinguished literary men, artists and musicians who shortly before 1600 gathered in the palace of the Count Bardi in Florence to discuss the possibilities of a new musical style.

When Don Carlo Gesualdo was a young boy his father had a camerata in their home in Venosa similar to the one in Florence.

Cantata—A composition for chorus and soloists in several movements that includes arias, duets, trios, etc. and chorales. It is usually accompanied by instruments.

Canzoni—Originally vocal music written to special poems very much like the madrigals. During the seventeenth century the canzoni were mostly written for instruments and were in the style of the later fugues.

Catches—English rounds of the seventeenth and eighteenth centuries written for three or more unaccompanied voices. First, one singer started and then each succeeding singer was to take up or "catch" his part at the right time. Sometimes, as in Purcell's catches, the words were so funny that the men had to stop singing because they were laughing so much.

Chaconne—A sixteenth century moderately slow dance of

Spanish origin written with three beats to the measure and an accent on the second beat.

During the Baroque Period the chaconne was written for instruments such as the organ, harpsichord and violin. It was still in a moderately slow tempo with three beats to the measure and an accent on the second beat but it was written in a more elaborate style. It consisted of a series of variations above a theme in the bass of not over eight measures, known as the "ground bass."

Chorale—The Hymn tunes of the German Protestant Church. These tunes were most important in German Baroque music. Buxtehude used them not only for vocal works but also as the basis for organ compositions. He wrote choral preludes, choral fugues, choral variations and choral fantasias.

Chromaticism—This occurs when a composer uses notes in a work that are not the ones in the regular major and minor scale of the key in which the piece is written. For example, in the key of C major there are no sharps or flats. But chords with F♯ or D♯ or any other note that is not in the scale is used even though it does not belong to the key of C major.

Colossal Baroque—Huge choral works for many singers accompanied by instruments.

Concerto Grosso—Popular form of concerto of the Baroque Period. Usually written in four movements for several solo instruments and orchestra. The part for solo instruments called *Concertino* or *Principale*. Parts for full orchestra called *Concerto* or *Tutti*.

Consort—A seventeenth century term for groups of instruments playing together as well as for compositions written for such groups.

Counterpoint—The art of combining two or more melodies in such a way that although they are played together each one can be heard separately.

Courante—A dance that originated in France in the sixteenth century and which, in the middle of the seventeenth century, became one of the movements in a suite.

There are two distinct types of courante:

I. *The Italian Corrente,* a rapid constantly moving dance with three beats to the measure.

II. *The French Courante,* also with three beats to the measure but slower than the *Italian Corrente.*

Double stops—The sounding together of two notes on an instrument of the violin family.

Fantasia—A piece in which a composer lets his fancy rove as it will. However, in the fantasias of the sixteenth and seventeenth centuries composers did follow set rules of counterpoint.

Fifths—Notes that have five tones apart in a scale such as c-g-d-a and so on. *Consecutive fifths* mean one fifth following the other.

Forte—To play or sing loudly. The abbreviation is f.

Fugue—A composition in which there are several parts or voices. A fugue is built on a melody called a subject. First the subject is announced by itself and then it is imitated in the other voices one after the other. Whenever a new voice plays the subject, the other voices play something else.

Gavotte—A seventeenth century dance originating in France and performed in a moderate tempo. There are four beats to a measure and it begins on the second half of the measure, which is the third beat.

The gavotte came into fashion when Lully introduced it into his ballets. It later became a movement in a suite.

Gigue—A lively dance developed from the sixteenth century Irish or English Jig.

During the late sixteenth and seventeenth centuries German, French and Italian composers wrote gigues. These were written in a variety of time signatures, such as 3/8, 6/8, 12/8, and sometimes 4/4 and the measures usually consisted of a long note followed by a short one. This idea of long, short; long, short; gives the sound of a "merry limp." Because of the lively character of the gigue it became the appropriate last movement of a suite.

Ground bass—A tune of four or eight measures in the bass that is repeated over and over again. It is the bass line for the melodies and harmonies written above it. The ground bass was particularly popular in the seventeenth century.

Harmony—The study of making chords and the way in which one chord is related to another. A chord is built by using three, four or more notes which are sounded together.

Hornpipe—A dance popular in England from the sixteenth through the nineteenth centuries. Many hornpipes were composed in the seventeenth and eighteenth centuries. These were usually written with four beats to the measure and with snappy rhythms and are found especially in the music of Purcell. In the nineteenth century the hornpipe became a popular solo dance for sailors.

Inversion—A chord is inverted when any note other than the root is the lowest note of the chord.

Kapellmeister—A German word for a musical director or for one who is in charge of music in a choir or an orchestra.

Largo—A broad and dignified tempo. Largo is considered to be the slowest of all the tempo marks.

Madrigal—A secular vocal composition for two or more voices set to a special poem.

Mass—A composition for voices, usually accompanied by instruments, based on the ritual of the Roman Catholic Church.

Minuet—An early French dance with three beats in the measure and in moderate speed. One of Lully's minuets became the official dance at the Court of Louis XIV.

Modulation—When a composer introduces modulations he is changing the key in which the piece is written. For example, he may begin a piece in C major, modulate to F major and then return to the original key. This is generally accomplished by a skillful use of chords.

Motet—A sacred vocal composition in contrapuntal style without instrumental accompaniment.

During the Baroque Period the organ and sometimes other instruments were used to accompany the voices.

Odes—A poem in free form. Composers wrote music for these poems which are usually in several sections of movements for chorus, soloist and orchestra.

Purcell wrote many odes for all sorts of occasions.

Opera—A story set to music for singers and orchestra. An opera is intended to be performed on a stage with scenery and costumes.

Oratorio—A composition for vocal solos, chorus, and instrumental accompaniment. It generally tells a story, and is almost always based on a religious theme. An oratorio is sung without costumes, acting or scenery.

Ordres—A form of suite written by Couperin. Instead of using the names of the dance forms such as allemande, courante, sarabande, gigue, etc., Couperin used descriptive titles for each movement, such as "The Mysterious Barricades," "The Satyrs," "The Windmill," etc.

Ornaments—The extra little notes, such as grace notes, trills, turns, etc. played or sung to decorate a melody. Sometimes they were written out by the composer but other times they were put in by the performer.

There were many ornaments used in the music of the Baroque Period.

Overture—Instrumental music played as an introduction to an opera or a musical play.

Lully was the first composer to have his overtures set the mood for the entire opera. Before that overtures were merely short pieces of music designed to quiet the audience.

Passacaglia—A piece of music written in the same way as a Chaconne. (See *Chaconne*)

Passepied—A gay quick French dance usually in 3/8 time. It was a great favorite in the Court of Louis XIV and Louis XV.

Passion Music—The musical settings of the text of the Passion, according to the four evangelists, Matthew, Luke, Mark and John.

Piano—To play or sing softly. The abbreviation is p.

Pizzicato—Plucking the strings of instruments instead of drawing the bow across them.

Monteverdi was the first composer to use pizzicato.

Prelude—A short composition sometimes used to prepare a listener for other music.

Buxtehude was the first composer to use "Prelude and Fugue" together.

Presto—A very fast tempo even faster than Allegro but slower than Prestissimo.

Program Music—Music inspired by a special story or poem expressing the ideas of the story in the music. For example, Vivaldi's four violin concertos "The Seasons."

Psalm—A sacred song set to the poems of the Book of Psalms in the Bible.

Schütz's first important work was his setting of the "Psalms of David."

Quodlibet—A humorous piece of music which includes snatches of well known popular melodies. Several melodies are played together at the same time.

Recitative—A style of singing which imitates and emphasizes the natural inflections of speech. It had its beginnings in about 1600 with the discovery of opera. It was used to carry on the story from one aria, duet or chorus to another.

Recitatives are also found in oratorios.

Ricercari—A form of music which came before the fugue but was written much in the same way with several parts or voices.

Ricercari were first written as vocal compositions but in the seventeenth century they were composed for the organ as well as for other instruments.

Rigaudon—A lively French dance with a jumping step which was originally a peasant dance of the seventeenth century. However, it also became a great favorite of Lully, Rameau and Purcell and they used the rigaudon in their ballets and operas.

Root—The lowest note of a chord. For example if a chord is C-E-G, the C is the root.

Rubato—means "robbed." To steal a little from the tempo by playing some phrases faster but to give back what was stolen by playing the next measures slower.

Frescobaldi was the first composer to introduce rubato into music.

Sarabande—A slow stately dance of the seventeenth and eighteenth century, originally from Spain. It was written with three beats to the measure and with an accent on the second beat. The sarabande became a slow movement in the suite and was usually placed just before the gigue.

Scherzo—A lively humorous piece. In Italian, scherzo means joke. In the Baroque Period the term scherzo was used especially for vocal pieces in a lighter style. As for example Monteverdi's "Scherzi Musicali."

Suite—An important instrumental form of Baroque Music consisting of a number of movements such as allemande, courante, minuet, gavotte, sarabande and gigue. Each movement is in the character of a dance and all are in the same key.

Tafelmusik—(Table Music) Music written to be played or sung for private or official dinners. Telemann wrote "Tafelmusik."

Toccatas—Intricate and difficult instrumental pieces that "show off" both the performers and the composers.

Tremolo—The quick repetition of the same tone which is produced by the very, very fast up and down movement of the bow on the strings of the instrument. This gives the feeling of trembling.

Monteverdi was the first composer to use the tremolo.

Trio sonata—The most important type of Baroque chamber music. It was written in three parts, two upper ones and a supporting bass. The trio sonata was performed by one, two, or four instruments, but never by three.

Word Painting—A style of writing in which the music followed the words. For example, if the words were "An angel ascended to Heaven," the music ascended higher and higher with the words.

Gesualdo was the first composer to use word painting in music.